LITERATURE AND THE ARTS
IN TWENTIETH CENTURY CHINA

A. C. SCOTT has spent more than twelve years in the Far East, in addition to four years' war service with the Royal Air Force in India and the Southeast Asia theatre. From 1946–49 he was on the staff of the British Council for Cultural Relations in Nanking, and he was there when the Communists took over the city. While in Nanking he was also an honorary visiting lecturer in fine arts in Hsü Pei-hung's old department in the National Central University. From 1950–52 he was with the Hong Kong office of the Council, and from 1952–54 he was in Japan. In 1956 he visited Peking especially to meet Mei Lan-fang and Ch'eng Yen-ch'iu and to make a general survey of the theatre and theatre schools. In 1957 he visited Taiwan as a member of a government-invited group from Hong Kong University, and while there had a special meeting with Ch'i Ju-shan. In 1958 a Rockefeller travel grant took him to Japan for three months to do research on the puppet theatre. From 1960 to autumn 1962 he was a staff member of the Men and Politics in Modern China research project at Columbia University. In autumn 1961 he directed a Chinese theatre workshop for the Institute of Advanced Studies in the Theatre Arts, New York. He has now joined the China Program at Cornell University. He is the author of several books, including *The Classical Theatre of China* and *Mei Lan-fang, Leader of the Pear Garden.*

Literature and the Arts
in Twentieth Century China

BY
A. C. SCOTT

Anchor Books
Doubleday & Company, Inc.
Garden City, New York

Anchor Books Edition: 1963

75127

CONTENTS

PREFACE

A book that attempts to survey as wide a field as this one must necessarily be drastic in selection while trying to remain informative. In the case of the personalities discussed, I have mentioned not only what appears most relevant about their work and background but often intrinsically unimportant details which seem to convey the atmosphere of the period, for it is a general picture of a period that is aimed at here. Such a treatment must be inadequate for the specialist, but if that were a reason for silence the ordinary reader would never be served.

I am deeply grateful to the following people for their assistance, advice, and encouragement in a number of ways. Mr. Ned Ouyang of the Mi Chou Gallery, New York; Mrs. Li Yu-ning of Columbia University; Professor Shen Hsüeh-yung, National Taiwan Academy of Arts; Mr. Lucian Wu, National Taiwan University; Dr. Liu Tsun-yan, Northcote Training College, Hong Kong; Mr. Kwok On, Hong Kong; Miss Hu Tieh, Hong Kong; Miss Rosie Wei, Hong Kong; Mr. Howard L. Boorman, Director, Modern China Project, Columbia University; and Mr. Howard Linton, East Asian Library, Columbia University. I must also thank Mr. Robert Payne for his permission to use the quotation from the poem by T'ien Chien on p. 30, and lastly my wife for her assistance at all times.

A. C. Scott

New York, 1962

WRITERS AND POETS DISCUSSED IN CHAP. II

AI CH'ING (1916–). Poet who became a Communist but was expelled by the Party in 1958.

CHAO SHU-LI (1903–). Communist writer of peasant stock.

CHENG CHEN-TO (1898–). Literary critic and historian. Founder of Society for Literary Research, 1921.

HSÜ CHIH-MO (1896–1931). Poet and member of the New Moon Group.

HU FENG. Communist literary critic who was the principal figure in a notorious Party denunciation in 1955.

HU SHIH (1891–1962). Scholar and writer. The leading figure of the Literary Revolution.

KU HUNG-MING (1865–1927). A Western-trained scholar and writer who continued to uphold the Chinese tradition even to the extent of retaining his queue.

KUO MO-JO (1892–). Poet, dramatist, archaeologist, and revolutionary. A guiding star of the Creation Society, 1922.

LAO SHE (SHU CH'ING-CH'UN, 1897–). Novelist, short-story writer, and dramatist.

LU HSÜN (CHOU SHU-JEN, 1881–1936). Essayist, critic, short-story writer, and art connoisseur. A key literary figure. Regarded by the Communists as the "father" of modern writing.

MAO TUN (SHEN YEN-PING, 1896–). Novelist and short-story writer. Now the Minister of Culture in China.

PA CHIN (LI FEI-KAN, 1904–). Novelist and short-story writer.

PING HSIN (1902–). Woman writer.

SHEN TS'UNG-WEN (1903–). Novelist and short-story writer.

T'IEN CHIEN. Contemporary poet.

TING LING (1907–   ). Woman writer. Expelled by the Communist party in 1958.

WEN I-TO (1899–1946). Poet and scholar. Key figure of New Moon Group. He was assassinated.

ACTORS AND DRAMATISTS DISCUSSED IN CHAP. III

CH'EN PAI-CH'EN (1907–   ). Dramatist and writer.

CHU HSÜ-TUNG. One of the founders of the early dramatic group, The Enlightenment Society (K'ai-ming-she).

HSIA YEN (SHEN TUAN-HSIEN, 1900–   ). Dramatist.

HSIUNG FO-HSI (1900–   ). Dramatist and teacher.

JEN T'IEN-CHIH. One of the founders of the Shanghai Spring Willow Society, 1907.

LI CHÜN-CHIU. One of the founders of The Enlightenment Society.

MEI LAN-FANG (1894–1961). The leading player of women's roles in the traditional Peking theatre; he visited the United States in 1930.

OU-YANG YÜ-CH'IEN (1887–   ). An actor in both the modern and traditional style theatres, he has also been playwright, film scriptwriter, producer, and teacher, and is one of the most versatile figures in the history of the modern theatre.

SUNG CHIH-TI (1914–   ). Dramatist.

TAI AI-LIEN (1916–   ). Pioneer of the modern dance movement; she is now head of the Peking Dance School.

T'IEN HAN (1898–   ). Dramatist and theatre specialist. Moving spirit of the South China Society and a pioneer of the modern stage movement.

TING HSI-LIN (1893–   ). A scientist and amateur dramatist whose one-act plays are famous.

TS'AO YÜ (1910–   ). The foremost modern dramatist, but he has produced nothing significant since 1949.

WANG CHUNG-SHENG. One of the founders of the Spring Willow Society, 1907.

YÜ SHANG-YUAN (1897–   ). One-time head of The National Dramatic Academy, Nanking.

CINEMA PERSONALITIES DISCUSSED IN CHAP. IV

CHANG SHIH-CH'UAN. Partner in the early Hsin Min Motion Picture Co., 1913.

CHAO TAN. Veteran film actor still active on the mainland.

CH'EN YUN-SHANG. A popular screen actress during the late thirties and early forties.

CHENG CHENG-CH'IU. Partner in the Hsin Min Motion Picture Co., 1913; later a director in the Star Motion Picture Co.

CHENG CHUN-I. Directed the 1960 film *Lin Tse-hsü*, a picture about the Opium War. It was shown in Europe.

CHING SAN. Director of the Communist film *Storm* made in 1959.

HU TIEH (BUTTERFLY WU, 1907?–   ). The *doyenne* of Chinese screen actresses. Still active in Hong Kong.

HUANG SHA. A director of *Liang Shan-po and Chu Ying-t'ai*, the first Communist colour-feature film shown in Europe (1955).

HUNG SHEN (1893–1955). Dramatist, actor, and film scriptwriter and director. A leading film personality of the thirties.

KU LAN-CHÜN (VIOLET KOO). Screen actress popular in the late thirties and early forties.

LO, T. Y. Director of the Nationalist China Motion Picture Corporation.

PAI YANG. *Doyenne* of screen actresses on the mainland. Rose to fame in the late thirties.

SANG HU. Co-director of the film *Liang Shan-po and Chu Ying-t'ai*.

TAN TU-YU. Director of the Shanghai Motion Picture Company, 1920.

TSENG FAN. Co-director of the 1960 film *Lin Tse-hsü*.

WAN LAI-MING, KU-CHAN, CHAO-CHEN, (brothers). Pioneers of the cartoon film in China.

WANG YÜAN-LUNG (1903–60). One of the most popular early male stars. Active until his death.

YANG NAI-MEI. Popular screen actress of the twenties.

YIN MING-CHU. Screen actress, wife of Tan Tu-yu.

ARTISTS MENTIONED OR DISCUSSED IN CHAP. V

CHANG TA-CH'IEN (1899–). Traditional style painter.

CH'EN YEN-CH'IAO. Wood-engraver, contemporary.

CH'I PAI-SHIH (1863–1957). Traditional style painter.

FENG TZU-K'AI (1898–). Cartoonist and illustrator.

HSÜ PEI-HUNG (1895–1953). Western and traditional style painter.

HUANG YUNG-YÜ (1924–). Wood-engraver, illustrator, and painter.

KAO CHIEN-FU (1879–1951). Traditional style painter using "contemporary" subject matter.

KAO CH'I-FENG (1889–1933). Brother and disciple of Kao Chien-fu.

LIU HAI-SU (1895–). Western style painter and teacher who reverted to traditional style.

PA-TA SHAN-JEN (CHU TA, 1626–c.1705). An old master who has had a strong influence on a number of contemporary Chinese painters.

P'U JU (1887–). Traditional style painter and member of former Imperial family.

SHIH T'AO (TAO CH'I, 1630–c.1707). Another old master of comparable influence.

YEH CH'IEN-YÜ (1907–). Creator of *Mr. Wang and Little Ch'en*, a widely popular comic strip cartoon, and prominent illustrator.

YEH FU. Wood-engraver, contemporary.

ARCHITECTS AND SCULPTORS MENTIONED OR DISCUSSED IN CHAP. VI

HUA T'IEN-YU (1902–). Paris-trained sculptor.

LIANG SSU-CH'ENG (1901–). Architectural historian and Dean of the Architectural Department, Tsinghua University, Peking.

LIAO HSIA-HSUEH (1906–). Paris-trained sculptor.

LIU K'AI-CH'Ü (1904–). Paris-trained sculptor.

LU YEN-CHIH (–1928). Architect who designed the Sun Yat-sen mausoleum, Nanking.

POY G. LEE (1900–). Architect and assistant to Lu Yen-chih.

WANG LING-I (1909–). Paris-trained sculptor.

MUSICIANS MENTIONED OR DISCUSSED IN CHAP. VII

HSIAO YU-MEI (1884–1940). Music theorist and first Director of the Shanghai Conservatory of Music.

HSIEN HSING-HAI (1905–45). Communist composer.

HUANG TZU (1904–38). Song composer and professor of the Shanghai Conservatory of Music.

LI CHIN-HUI. Composer of "yellow music" in the thirties.

MA SZU-TS'UNG. Paris-trained violinist and director of the Central Conservatory of Music, Peking.

NIEH ERH (NIEH TZU-YI, 1912–35). Communist song writer and composer.

PERSONALITIES MENTIONED OR DISCUSSED IN CHAP. VIII

CHANG CH'ING-YING. Woman painter, resident in London.

CH'EN CH'I-K'UAN (1921–). Contemporary painter, resident in the United States. (At present, head of architectural department, Tung Hai University, Taiwan.)

CH'I JU-SHAN (1876–1962). Theatre scholar and specialist. Adviser to Mei Lan-fang, the actor.

CHIANG YEE (1903–). Author and illustrator, formerly resident in England, now in the United States.

CHOU WEN-CHUNG (1923–). Contemporary composer, resident in the United States.

FEI CH'ENG-WU. Painter and illustrator, resident in London. Husband of Chang Ch'ing-ying.

FU TS'UNG. Pianist, trained in Communist China but now resident in London.

HSIEH PING-YING (1908–). Woman revolutionary and author. Now resident in Taiwan.

HSIUNG SHIH-I (1902–). Author and dramatist, formerly resident in England, now in Hong Kong.

HSÜ TI-SHAN (1893–1941). Scholar and writer, professor of Chinese in Hong Kong University.

HUNG SIN-NUI. Contemporary actress in the Cantonese theatre, formerly of Hong Kong.

LIANG SHIH-CH'IU (1902–). Literary critic and translator of Shakespeare, now resident in Taiwan.

LIN YÜ-T'ANG (1895–). Novelist and journalist, resident in the United States.

LU PI-YÜN. Screen actress, Shanghai, and now, Taiwan.

MA SI-TSANG. Cantonese actor, formerly of Hong Kong, now on the mainland. Wife is Hung Sin-nui.

MENG YAO (YANG TSUNG-CHEN, 1919–). Woman writer, resident in Taiwan.

PEI IEOH MING (1917–). Contemporary architect, resident in New York.

RAN IN-TING (1902–). Taiwan painter.

SHEN HSÜEH-YUNG. Woman singer and director of the music department, National Academy of Arts and Crafts, Taiwan.

SU HSÜEH-LIN (1897–). Woman scholar and writer, now resident in Taiwan.

TENG, CESAR C. K. Violinist and director of the National Research Institute of Music, Taiwan.

TSENG YU-HO (1923–   ). Contemporary painter, now resident in Honolulu.

WANG LAN (1922–   ). Writer and official, Taiwan.

WONG, ANNA MAY (1907–61). Film star, born and worked in the United States.

ILLUSTRATIONS

LITERATURE AND THE ARTS
IN TWENTIETH CENTURY CHINA

I. THE BACKGROUND

The great arts in China have always been calligraphy, painting, and poetry. The ink-loaded brush symbolised the essence of Chinese culture. Painting and writing were interchangeable in that they required the same materials, ink, brush, and paper; a picture, a poem, and written characters were complementary forms. They were essentially the creations of a certain class, the scholars. By extension this meant those who governed. The first qualification of the old-style Chinese government official was that he be a man of letters, and recruitment for the civil service was by means of competitive literary examinations. This meant that all candidates had to be men versed in the arts. Owing to the nature of the Chinese language every educated man was skilled in calligraphy to some degree and therefore in the basic principle of painting technique, control of the brush. And since the scholar-officials were always a select minority in old China it is easy to see why the fine arts were always associated with social status.

This in turn meant that the amateur was regarded as the only true artist. The professional, the man who accepted payment for his artistic productions, if not actually despised was at any rate considered an inferior. The sculptor of religious figures, the performer on a musical instrument, were accepted as worthy craftsmen and performers but nothing more. The actor on the other hand was regarded as a social outcast and women entertainers as no better than courtesans. This concept of the arts persisted in Chinese minds until the structure of traditional society was changed by the revolution that in 1911 turned China

1

into a Republic. Even then the old attitudes lingered and were not easily effaced.

From 1644 to 1911 China was ruled by the Manchus, alien conquerors who had usurped the Chinese throne at Peking. The Manchus had little developed culture of their own—they were largely warriors and horsemen in the beginning—and so while reigning as the political masters they were content to let the great traditions of Chinese art and literature carry on. The mismanagement of a corrupt and reactionary Court finally brought the country into disastrous conflict with the aggressive industrialised Western powers, whose hands were strengthened by the failure of China's ultra-conservative administration to grasp the significance of a changing world beyond their own borders. From being a source of strength, China's backward-looking tradition became her greatest weakness, and revolution finally swept the monarchy away. On January 1, 1912, Dr. Sun Yat-sen, the rebel leader, a missionary-educated Cantonese and graduate of the Hong Kong Medical College, was proclaimed the first President of China.

During the Manchu period the traditional patterns of Chinese culture continued on repetitive lines without any great creative contributions. The more noteworthy achievements were in the fields of literary recording and compilation and in the encouragement of a popular theatre which had the patronage of the Manchu Court. With the decline of the dynasty and the corresponding disintegration of the old civilisation, the arts and literature, ingrown for such a long period of time, became increasingly sapped of vigour and stifled by conformity. The society of which they were the cultural reflection was one ruled by an elite in which men were not considered as equally endowed. No voice might be raised against the State with impunity. Civil rights were intentionally limited as a measure to ensure loyalty under the supreme personal control vested in the Emperor. All ranks of society were bound by a strict code of form and taboo in daily living. The family was sacrosanct, and nepotism was a recognised form of professional advancement. Women were allowed no part in public life and were subjugated under the system of arranged marriages which recognised concubinage as a domestic institution. And by the end of the Manchu period corruption had become tacitly "accepted" throughout the community.

This, broadly speaking, was the state of affairs against which the younger generation rebelled after 1911. They naturally used literature and the arts to show their renunciation of the past and determination to advance into a new age. In seeking a new artistic vision they needed the technical means to express it and so instinctively turned towards the West from which the winds of change had first blown.

The 1911 Revolution was never wholly successful in achieving its aim. It brought changes in the political and social system of China and created a climate for reform, but in the end its leaders were unable to form a strong central government or to eliminate many fundamental causes of unrest and corruption in the nation. Disillusion replaced the first flush of idealism. Nevertheless, for a time at least, the post-1911 period brought freedom for students and scholars to become acquainted with the ideas and methods of Western art, science, and literature in a way that had been impossible before. And although this period of eager intellectual experiment was eventually submerged beneath the political confusion and decentralisation into which Republican China was soon plunged, it was not before the social conscience of the younger generation had been aroused and their national pride in new cultural achievement stimulated. The impact of events was soon reflected in literature and the arts whose developments were complementary to the political and social evolution of the country. Modern Chinese poets, painters, novelists, and dramatists have served as recorders and in-

3

terpreters of the transfiguration of traditional society with its attendant and complex crop of human problems.

While being a mirror of social revolution and change, the artist himself has been assailed by a conflict of values: how best to retain his creative integrity and yet adjust it to the problems of a new age in China. The broad issues have been whether to discard Chinese traditions and follow Western techniques unconditionally, whether to compromise in searching for new artistic methods through a fusion of the two, or whether to remain simply and resolutely Chinese. This dilemma of adjustment between Eastern and Western creative methods has dominated the arts in China for fifty years, and no final solution has yet been possible. There has not been time, for what is fifty years when a culture thousands of years old is involved in readjustment? And the problem is further complicated today by the imposition of Marxist methodology in the arts.

Until 1949 modern Chinese literature probably achieved the most in its role as a sensitive recorder of the ebb and flow of contemporary social history. Painting, music, the theatre, and in a more limited sense, architecture, remained fields of experiment vacillating between past and present and often falling between the two stools. The cinema was still too new to achieve anything really advanced.

During the early years of the Republic, Chinese attempts to use Western art forms were often crudely imitative and nothing more. The lack of any true standards of critical approach and the need for youth to be fashionably "Western" at all costs produced some odd results. But once a number of Chinese writers and artists began to go abroad and study seriously, a more level-headed approach to Western arts developed. This in turn was followed by a period of sober re-appraisals. The conviction grew that following Western forms was not in itself an antidote to China's cultural malaise, any more than the outward assumption of "democratic" government was the solution to the nation's political ills. In fact the signs of cleavage

4

and confusion often seemed indicative to some that the arts in China had lost their way.

For many thinking people the issue became more complex. Their honeymoon with the West was over. The crisis in China's affairs brought about by continued civil war and political chicanery compelled many men and women to decide that the only test of a contemporary art movement was in its value to the political future of China. They felt that any modern art form could have vitality only through its close relationship with the people and their hopes. In other words, the supreme test of a new art for China was in its ideological content. The artist had to fulfil his political and social obligations in his work. And so a strong leftist movement arose among the artists and writers, although not all of them subscribed to the notion of political control of creative effort. Between the extremists who actively supported Marxist theory and the conservatives who advocated laissez-faire, there was a large body of "liberals" in the arts. While politically passive, they were socially indignant and highly conscious of the urgent need for a constructive approach to the problems of their country.

There were undeniable causes to justify the left viewpoint in the arts. The new intelligentsia in China was largely composed of men and women who had studied abroad, or at any rate received a Western-style education in their own country. But they were an urban minority. A large part of China's rural population could not read or write its own language, much less that of another country. Although Shanghai, Peking, and Canton were the centres of new developments in art and literature and the milieu of the *avant-garde* movement, these great cities represented an infinitesimal part of China, and some Western-educated Chinese tended to ignore this. It was one thing for intellectuals with a knowledge of other languages to adopt new methods in the arts; it was quite another to develop them within China so that they could have

5

meaning for a less intellectually privileged class of society.

In the theatre, for example, ordinary Chinese people brought up in the non-realistic traditions of their own stage could hardly be expected to show enthusiasm for Western-style dialogue-drama portraying psychological conflicts that were not even within their experience. This was only a facet of the vast problem confronting the new art prophets. A Chinese critic writing in a Shanghai weekly in 1938 expanded the theme as follows:

> One of the chief troubles with the Chinese new intelligentsia has always been the extreme pride and solicitude with which they regard their own prestige. Chinese students after graduation invariably go into politics, business, or academic circles for a career or living, but they would rather face unemployment and starvation than become an actor or a public entertainer, which they would consider as beneath their honour. If they come to write or paint they make it a point to choose their subject matter from what they represent as the highest standards of taste and cultural accomplishment, fearing that the least sign of vulgarity would drag them down from the respectable heights of scholarship. This perverted psychology is partly responsible for their estrangement from the masses. . . . *

This sharp indictment perhaps simplified the vices at the expense of the virtues. There were men who attempted to break with tradition and set up as independent dramatists, writers, or painters, but economic necessity, if nothing else, compelled them sooner or later to bow before the old idol of scholarly status. Teaching was the best way they could support their usually large families. Before 1949 it was desirable for any Chinese writer, painter, musician, or dramatist to have the dignity of a university title on his

* E. E. Liu, *The China Critic.*

visiting card. Most of the big names in modern Chinese arts and literature were in academic employment during their professional careers.

The fact that they depended on government institutions for their living tended to strengthen the hand of conformity by perpetuating the old scholarly status symbol in a modern guise, maintaining a rift between the intellectual and the community at large, and assisting political control of the arts.

The Sino-Japanese War (1937–45) solved the political dilemma of Chinese artists and writers drastically, at least for the duration. They were united in the common national cause of resistance to the Japanese. The great mass migration to West China, when thousands of the population fled before the enemy, materially affected not only geographical but class distinctions. It was no longer possible to speak of artists and writers being "estranged from the masses," they were one with them as they had never been before. Literature, music, theatre, and the graphic arts were devoted to arousing and sustaining the patriotic emotions of the ordinary people in the idioms they loved and understood. This meant a new approach on the part of the artists and writers and a greater understanding of the lives and character of the ordinary people with whom they now shared a common existence and aim.

In the first years of the struggle against the Japanese the theme of all the arts was proud defiance and romantic idealisation of the people's heroism in their struggle for the country's future. The life and death struggle was also seen as the re-forging period for the democratic China that up to then had existed in name only. But as the long war years dragged on with little alleviation of human suffering or social evils and continued corruption and political scheming in high places, a new mood of cynicism set in. Artists and writers were driven to more objective criticism and probing. By the sixth year of the war, for example, more than fifty plays had been banned by the

Nationalist Government on the grounds that they were pro-Communist, which meant largely that they exposed the government's failings too ruthlessly.

In February 1945, six months before the final day of victory over the Japanese, a cultural manifesto signed by three hundred leading intellectuals was presented to the Chungking government. Among the names were those of many men and women prominent in the arts and literature, and their despair was given expression in these words: ". . . in internal politics we have not achieved unity; in the government there is only corruption and bribery . . . cultural and educational fields suffer restrictions and oppression. . . ." It was a note of warning that went unheeded. When the Nationalist Government fled the mainland before the Communists in 1949 there were few tears shed among the writers and artists of China.

The retreat of the Nationalist Government to Taiwan caused a political and cultural division of a new kind. It also created a complex international problem and caused thousands of intellectuals and educated middle-class Chinese to emigrate to the various countries of Southeast Asia, South America, Europe, and the United States. The Chinese race is now spread across the earth in a new way and at a new level of intellectual society. The long involvement of modern Chinese art and literature with social revolution and political dogma still continues.

II. LITERATURE

A movement called the Literary Revolution was the turning point in modern China's cultural development after the political events of 1911. It began as a crusade for language reform and first gathered impetus in the spring of 1919, to become the driving force behind an ardent new generation determined to support social changes through Western concepts. These young people considered the classical Chinese language ill suited to the task of propagating new ideas. It was too indefinite in its usage and too limited in its audience to serve the spokesmen of a new age, and so a group of far-seeing intellectuals set about sponsoring a programme of literary reforms.

From early times written and spoken Chinese had been sharply divided in both style and syntax. An ability to write even moderately well demanded not only the mastery of thousands of characters drawn with a brush but a command of highly stylised prose dependent on abstruse historical allusions, a multiple system of governing particles, and other complexities of usage. Written Chinese was a scholar's medium in which perfection might be achieved only after long years of concentrated study. To the *lao-pai-hsing*, or common people, it was virtually a foreign language.

The conventions of Chinese literary style tended to make writers mere compilers or imitators of mannerisms; their work lacked the motive force of creative literature. Life for them was a well-ordered formula to be expressed as such; they were divorced from living society. Even before the 1911 Revolution a new and growing class of Western-

9

educated Chinese were beginning to criticise traditional literature on these grounds. The retarding influence of Confucianism was condemned for its remoteness from the social and political problems of the day. Full of new discoveries about the rights of man and the emancipation of women, youth demanded a literature concerned with the immediate task of living.

This was the spirit that fired the pioneers of the Literary Revolution. Among them was Hu Shih (1891–1962), a brilliant young scholar who, while at Columbia University in 1917, sent an epoch-making article, "Suggestions for a Reform of Literature," to *New Youth,* a magazine founded in 1915 that was to become the mouthpiece of the younger intellectuals. The editor was Ch'en Tu-hsiu (1879–1942), Dean of the School of Letters in Peking University and a veteran revolutionary. The university chancellor, Ts'ai Yüan-p'ei (1876–1940), was another staunch partisan of literary reform and an influential supporter of the arts, which he thought a vital substitute for religion in youthful minds. Yet another reformer was Ch'ien Hsuan-t'ung (1887–1939), a scholar sceptic who went to the extreme of demanding complete abolition of the old written language, a proposal the more rational Hu Shih argued was clearly impossible.

Even reformers must agree to differ, but the basic aim of these men was the same. They thought the new democracy meaningless unless the old literary hierarchy was abolished and universal education made possible. The first step towards these ends was to follow the colloquial method of speech in writing. This aroused strong opposition because the classical written language was revered by Chinese scholars rather as Latin and Greek had been by Western academics. Lin Shu (1852–1924), a prolific translator into literary Chinese of Scott, Dickens, Tolstoy, and many other Western authors, sent an open letter of protest to the Peking University chancellor demanding instant dismissal of faculty members who used the "cant of street vendors and

rickshaw pullers." His protests—and also those of Ku Hung-
ming (1856–1927), a European-educated member of the
university staff and an ardent apostle of traditional Chinese culture—were in vain. The younger intellectuals and
the students were solidly behind the reformers.

The battle was finally won in what was afterwards called
the May Fourth Movement of 1919. On this date the students of Peking rose in violent protest against the Chinese
government's acquiescence to the Versailles Treaty decision
that ceded former German territory in Shantung to Japan.
It was the first sign of a new intellectual class militantly
determined to have a voice in their country's affairs.

Following these demonstrations there appeared a growing number of little magazines printed in the colloquial
style and stating the case for Chinese youth. There were
soon hundreds of them, with titles like *New Tide, Young
China, New Society, The New Life*. The very names indicated the ardour of a generation dedicated to reform.
Many of the magazines were short-lived, and their literary
standards were uneven, but they provided a platform for
free intellectual debate of a kind previously unknown. And
their impact on the nation created a climate for lasting
reform. They were indeed the true heralds their titles proclaimed them.

One Chinese writer said of the period following the May
Fourth Movement: ". . . some twenty centuries of Western literature were compressed into a single moment to
quench the thirst of the new generation. There was something like Elizabethan profusion, something of the robust-
ness too, in the way the new works were produced. Girls
walked out of their homes to tread the independent path
of Ibsen's Nora while young men with dishevelled hair
and pale faces, and above all a seriousness that beat down
every obstacle, began to form clubs and societies which
had a mushroom growth all over China. 'Bliss was it in
that dawn to be alive, But to be young was very heaven!'"

An important offshoot of the new literary movement

was the Society for Literary Research, founded in Peking in January 1921. This was a loosely organised group whose manifesto called for new writing dedicated to humanity instead of literary effect, the translation of Western authors, and new standards of criticism. Cheng Chen-to (1898–), a literary historian, was the founder with twelve other members. They were fortunate in being offered the monopoly of a well-established miscellany, *The Short Story Magazine*, published by the Commercial Press in Shanghai. It served as the Society's journal and between the years 1921 and 1931 published the work of practically every important new writer and so encouraged a tradition of contemporary fiction.

A second important literary group of the period was the Creation Society formed by a group of students who had studied in Japan. They attracted public notice in May 1922 when they published the first number of a quarterly entitled *Creation*. A guiding star of the group was Kuo Mo-jo (1892–) who had graduated in medicine but abandoned it for literature. Poet, dramatist, archaeologist, and finally revolutionary, Kuo had many talents of which more will be said later.

The Creation Society began as romantics, individualists, and in one or two cases, decadents. They admired Byron, Shelley, and Keats, whose works they translated. Shelley's passionate involvement in revolutionary issues and Byron's revolt against society and sympathy for Greek insurgents awoke responsive chords in the Creation group, which suggests a link between their early romanticism and later political spirit. The factions that eventually developed in the modern Chinese literary movement were numerous, but every conscientious writer was in his own way inspired by revolution in the broader sense. Each was concerned with building a new society.

The Creation Society remained an influential organisation until February 1929, when it was proscribed by the government. By then it had passed through changes of membership and outlook, although Kuo Mo-jo remained a dominating figure to the end. In the final phase he was an advocate of the proletarian revolutionary cause then gaining momentum.

The Creation Society and the Society for Literary Research were rivals who often attacked each other's ideas, but both were signposts of the first decisive period of the new literary movement. Both were equally the product of an era of assimilation and realisation, when the passionate and often confused ideals of Chinese middle-class youth gained a public hearing, and the resounding Western principles of liberty, fraternity, and equality were flaunted in defiance of Confucian controls. Despite the artificiality and imitativeness of much of their work, the period saw great cultural and social changes in the cities, although an illiterate majority elsewhere remained unaffected by trends that were primarily the concern of a class educated in Japan or the West.

When the first number of the *Creation Quarterly* was published at Shanghai in 1922, a great Chinese seamen's strike had just ended in British-controlled Hong Kong to the far south. By immobilising the famous entrepôt the seamen paralysed colonial trade and so gained the first major victory over Western discrimination against Chinese workers. In 1925 there was another big outburst in Shanghai. Incidents arising out of strikes among Chinese workers in textile mills and the fatal firing on student demonstrators by the British-led police, angered the whole Chinese community. Intellectuals, workers, household servants, even the sing-song girls, applauded by word and deed a movement to free their country from hated foreign domination. Communist headquarters seized upon the opportunity to stir the boiling pot, but the fact remains that national pride had reached breaking point among the Chinese. They were tired of the superior attitudes of the West.

In 1926 a great military campaign to unite China was launched from Canton under Chiang Kai-shek's command.

Several men later famous in the literary field took part as members of the education-propaganda corps. The campaign's success, however, was synonymous with an increased Communist control of the labour unions, a lasting split in the Nationalist Government party, and the severing of diplomatic relations with Russia. Many patriotic idealists emerged disillusioned, but Chiang arose as the military saviour of China backed by a powerful right-wing clique.

In 1927 a ruthless *coup d'état* placed Shanghai under the control of the extreme rightist Nationalist party led by Chiang Kai-shek and paved the way for military dictatorship posing as democracy and basically supported by merchants, financiers, and entrepreneurs. The new regime's cultural ideals were a synthesis of neo-Confucianism with its politico-private patronage and active suppression of free speech, implemented by the initiation of the Communist "witch-hunt" as a method of "nationalising" artistic expression. The 1927 events brought to a climax long years of political squabbling and civil war in a China divided and demoralised by the failure of the 1911 Revolution to produce a strong central government. The revolutionaries had become sadly split among themselves, war lords had run riot throughout the land, and Russia had advanced her own interests by exploiting the nationalistic fervour against Western extraterritorial controls.

The complexities of this political jigsaw puzzle are not for discussion here. It suffices to say that by 1927 a large body of Chinese artists and writers had been disillusioned. The failure of the middle classes to consolidate their social revolution was finally driven home. New and powerful currents within Chinese society began to affect the intellectuals. The artistic emotionalism of an earlier period became fused with more positive attitudes on national issues and complicated by the spread of Marxist ideas among literary men. The changing situation was summed up by Kuo Mo-jo in later years when he wrote: ". . . the demands of society did not permit us to remain enclosed within ivory towers any longer . . . we sensed the need for change but had no power to enforce it. . . ."

In February 1930 the League of Left-wing Writers was founded under the sponsorship of the writer Lu Hsün supported by some fifty novelists, poets, and dramatists. It became a rallying point for many younger writers and, at the same time, the centre of many literary-political disputes and quarrels. The Nationalist Government's persecution of leftist writers only added fuel to the flames in a period over which lurked the menace of Japan's war preparations.

In 1931 the Japanese seizure of Manchuria outraged Chinese national feelings. When fighting took place in Shanghai in 1932, the result of vicious reprisals against a Chinese boycott of Japanese trade, many writers needed no further convincing that their country demanded their first allegiance. But there was a lull before the storm, a minor golden age of artistic activities in Shanghai before full-scale aggression burst upon China in 1937 and the nation's writers moved to create a common front against the enemy. Literary-political affiliations were temporarily forgotten by some, while others made their choice and moved to Communist headquarters at Yenan. But patriotism was a dominating theme for all during the long war years.

The spirit of unity encouraged by national emergency withered and vanished altogether in the bitter post-war era whose social and economic chaos ended in the rout of a weak government and Communist seizure of power. With few exceptions the country's writers stayed on to work under the new regime. Their attitude was that nothing could be worse than conditions had been under the Nationalists. It was a point of view shared by painters, actors, and musicians as well. There certainly was trepidation about the new rulers in many cases, but the Nationalist Government had long ago forfeited its mandate as far as the arts were concerned.

Writers already sympathetic to the extreme left welcomed the Communist cultural programme with great expectations, although not all of them were destined to remain in Party favour. Literature became a very different political weapon from the one conceived by certain once-enthusiastic protagonists of proletarian revolution. But these matters are treated later. Having now sketched in the broad phases of the modern literary movement it is time to consider some typical writers.

THE WRITERS

The work of the following writers by no means provides a complete coverage of modern Chinese literary history, although several of the better-known figures are included here. But the work of all of them, however varied in style and technique, reflects their common concern with an age of social protest, conflicting ethical values, and the emotional frustrations of a younger generation confronted with a changing world.

An outstanding literary social critic was Lu Hsün (1881–1936) who came from a scholarly Chekiang family and whose real name was Chou Shu-jen. Lu Hsün has become a political cult in Communist China, though no one would be more surprised than he to see how his name is now used in the cause of literary conformity, for he was a passionate individualist in his work. And setting aside the propaganda verbiage, he remains a towering personality as an essayist, critic, and short-story writer who exerted a powerful effect on the literary and social life of China.

Lu Hsün received a sound classical Chinese education before studying Western medicine in Japan, and took up literature as his profession. His astringent essays, published in the press, attacked official corruption, outmoded social customs, in fact the whole fabric of Chinese society whose weaknesses moved him to anger. He wanted China to take her rightful place in the world community. In his short stories he had a satiric style that was unique and therefore immensely effective. Echoes of the old elegant tradition were combined with a studied Western structure. Unfortunately his stylistic mannerisms are lost in translation, for Lu Hsün excelled in a *double entendre* that can be created only by skilful juxtaposition of Chinese characters. Almost lyrical in his softer moments, Lu Hsün never forgot his avowed purpose, to attack. Literature was his weapon.

The most widely known of Lu Hsün's works is probably "The True Story of Ah Q," a long short story that has achieved an international reputation and from which both a film and a play have been made in China. Though by no means Lu Hsün's masterpiece, the story is a typically sharp commentary on the failings of post-1911 society, epitomised in the miserable career of Ah Q, a nameless odd-job man without background or education, but full of the conceits of his superiors whose ineffectiveness and bullying he emulates in his own actions.

Thrown out of his employer's home for speaking amorously to a maidservant, Ah Q leaves the district to fraternise with thieves. He returns to sell stolen goods in his old neighbourhood which he attempts to terrorise by pretending to be a revolutionary in an effort to gain prestige. Arrested by genuine revolutionaries who enter the town, he is shot for a crime of which he is innocent. The story ends: "Naturally, all agreed that Ah Q had been a bad man, the proof being that he had been shot; for if he had not been bad how could he have been shot? But the opinion in the town was unfavourable. Most people were dissatisfied, thinking a shooting was not such a fine spectacle as a decapitation; and what a ridiculous culprit he had been, too, to have passed through so many streets without singing a line from an opera. They had followed him for nothing."

In Ah Q, Lu Hsün satirised national defects. The odd-job man's words were ambivalent and his actions indecisive yet he was "forever contented." His creator ironically pointed out that this was overwhelming evidence "why China's spiritual courtesy was supreme in the world." Within his foolish person Ah Q the underdog symbolised the spirit of political failure of China's transitional period. Lu Hsün saw the Chinese people as a nation of Ah Qs confined in an "iron house without windows" and being suffocated to death without knowing it. He wanted to awaken an "agonising awareness of imminent death."

"The True Story of Ah Q" was first published in 1923 in a collection of short stories entitled *Call to Arms* wherein Lu Hsün attempted to dissect the national dilemma whose urgency and tragedy were first brought home to him as a student in Japan. There he had seen an early film of the execution of an alleged Chinese spy during the Russo-Japanese War (1904–5). He was shocked because fellow Chinese students remained unmoved by the film. "Consequently," he said afterwards, "I tried through various means to anaesthetize my soul. . . ." Lu Hsün's bitterness of spirit sprang from a great compassion for his own people.

Mao Tun, the present Minister of Culture in China, was a writer both professionally and politically close to Lu Hsün. (The past tense is used because since 1949 he has produced no new work.) Mao Tun is the pen name of Shen Yen-ping, born in Chekiang province in 1896. He began as a proofreader in the Commercial Press, Shanghai, and was promoted to editor of *The Short Story Magazine* when it became the organ of the Society for Literary Research, of which he was a founding member. He developed into one of China's leading novelists, with a flair for plot and unadorned narration that showed him a master of uncompromising realism.

Mao Tun's reputation was made with a trilogy called *Eclipse* published in 1927. It described student participation in the Nationalist military campaign of 1926, in which the author took part as a propaganda officer. *Disillusionment, Dilemma,* and *Pursuit,* the three titles of the trilogy, indicate Mao Tun's feelings. His account of the love affairs of a college girl turned revolutionary was a starting point for the theme that revolution is meaningless if the people do not first understand its true aim.

Midnight, Mao Tun's second major novel, published in 1933, was inspired by Shanghai big business and showed the futility of China's new industries faced with foreign competition and control. The book has been hailed in Communist China as his masterpiece. Among all the novelists sympathetic to the extreme left Mao Tun was artistically outstanding. He had deep psychological perception and was one of the few writers who treated a love story objectively and with understanding. His writings sensitively convey the emotional conflicts of young people during the stormy years of revolution. Less passionate and less bitter than Lu Hsün, he nevertheless used satire a great deal, even to the point of caricature. Besides writing stories and novels he was a versatile translator and editor.

Shen Ts'ung-wen, born in Hunan in 1903 of a military family, was a very different kind of writer. Popular and prolific in his early days, he was nicknamed the "Dumas of China." He had a colourful career. After only a primary school education he enlisted as an ordinary soldier in 1916. He served chiefly in West China where he became a regimental clerk. In 1923 he left the army to try his hand at writing in Peking. Encouraged by Hu Shih and others, he began writing stories about army life, the ordinary people he had met in West China, and the Miao tribespeople whom he knew well, for he had tribal blood in his own veins from his maternal grandmother.

Many of his Miao tales had an idyllic quality that appealed especially to young people. His style was vigorous and simple and conveyed a sense of adventure that made people ask for more. Shen's output was tremendous in his day: by 1934 he had written thirty-five volumes. Later, however, he entered academic life and his style tended to become more elaborate. But primarily he was a story-teller and at his best in his simple tales of his early life.

He mixed with a bohemian literary set in Peking and met the woman writer Ting Ling whom he introduced to his friend Hu Yeh-p'in, a would-be writer. Hu married Ting Ling and with Shen they set up a *ménage à trois* in Shanghai where they became a favourite subject of gossip in the twenties. They ran their own publishing firm, which failed because of financial mismanagement. Shen took a university post, while Hu entered active politics. Hu was arrested in 1931 and executed as a Communist by the Nationalist police. Shen made a vain attempt to plead for his friend's life in Nanking, for although he considered Hu's politics misguided he remained personally loyal when many progressive friends kept silent.

Shen suffered greatly when the Communists came to power in 1949 and even tried to commit suicide. He recovered to make his peace with the regime, ironically enough shortly before his former companion, Ting Ling, who had previously denounced Shen as bourgeois, was purged from the party and banished to manual labour.

Ting Ling, born in 1907, and like Shen a Hunanese, was a greatly discussed writer, as much for her personal life during the late twenties and early thirties as for her political downfall later. The daughter of a well-to-do family, Ting Ling attended a Shanghai girl's school known for its "progressive" leanings and from there entered the Communist-influenced Shanghai University, noted for the personal freedom it allowed its students. In 1924 she went to Peking and began her literary career by having a story published in *The Short Story Magazine*.

Her early work was noted for its unabashed treatment of sex and women's emotional problems. Her story, "Diary of Miss Sophie," published in the late twenties and reportedly autobiographical, caused a furore in its day. So did another story, "Wei Hu," which dealt with the sexual incompatibility of people with different levels of political awareness. In 1932, Ting Ling joined the Communist party and after that wrote about soldiers, peasants, and the usual revolutionary themes. Her last achievement in this genre was *The Sun Shines over the Sangkan River*, a dull novel about land reform which was awarded the Stalin Prize for literature in 1951.

Politically, the wheel has come full circle for Ting Ling. Between 1933–36 she was imprisoned by the Nationalist authorities, but escaped to the Communist areas when she was released on parole. She played a prominent part in Communist political-literary activities until 1957 when she was sensationally expelled from the party in Peking and set to scrubbing floors as punishment for her rightism. In a *History of Modern Chinese Literature* published by the Foreign Languages Press in Peking in 1959, she is dismissed in two words: "bourgeois writer." No mention is made of her work or her party connections.

A very different woman writer is Ping Hsin, born in Fukien in 1902, who had a considerable following among young people in the twenties. She came from a comfortable middle-class family and was a precocious reader as a child. She learned to write classical poetry and while still a university student in Peking contributed stories to the literary supplement of that city's *Morning Post* and to *The Short Story Magazine*. After graduating, she went to the United States and entered Wellesley College where she wrote a series called *Letters to My Little Readers*, which described life in America and became very popular with Chinese children.

Ping Hsin's early stories described the younger generation in a period of national transition, but her later work became increasingly sentimental with a constant harping on the philosophy of universal love. Her output was small, mostly short stories, essays, or poetry, the best of which conveyed a sensitive interpretation of youthful ideals and dreams in the sentimental tradition that has always existed in China. Ping Hsin is married and today works as a children's propaganda specialist in Peking.

Neither of these two women can be regarded as a major artist, but both are unique in their period and represent some of the byways of the modern literary movement. Two major writers who deserve attention are Pa Chin and Lao She, each in his own way a master of the novel.

Pa Chin is the pen name of Li Fei-kan, born in 1904. He came from a wealthy West China family whose household numbered close to one hundred persons with the servants, a complex hierarchy of personalities that inspired some of his most famous stories. After studying English and French in Chengtu, Pa Chin went to Shanghai where he became deeply interested in the Western anarchist movement with which he retained connections for many years. In 1927 he went to Paris and wrote his first novel *Destruction* which was published serially in *The Short Story Magazine*. It is a romantic tragedy whose young hero, embittered by his sweetheart's acceptance of her parents' choice of husband, dedicates his thwarted affections to the cause of the downtrodden and embarks on political activities. These end in the attempted assassination of a police chief and his own execution. The novel made Pa Chin's literary reputation, and on his return from Paris he took up writing as a career.

Probably his best-known book is *Family*, the first volume of a trilogy called *The Torrent*. A saga of wealthy middle-class life, which the author knew so well, its plot is woven round the marriage problems and frustrated love affairs of the children of a large West China household. Chüeh-hui, the youngest of three brothers, is a rebel against family tradition and customs. He falls in love with a pretty maidservant, Ming-feng, who, unknown to him, is promised as a concubine to an old reprobate. On the eve of her departure, she goes tearfully to her lover's room, but he is engrossed in writing and after kissing her for the first time asks her to leave, saying that he will talk with her in two days' time. In despair she goes from his room and drowns herself in the lake:

> As Ming-feng left Chüeh-hui's room she knew this time all hope was gone. She was sure he loved her as much as ever. His kiss was still warm on her lips and she still felt the clasp of his hand. These things proved that he loved her but they also emphasised the fact that she was going to lose him and be given to a lecherous old man. She would never see him again. There would only be pain and sorrow in the long years ahead. Why cling to a life like that? Why remain where there was no love? . . . She went straight to the garden, groping her way with difficulty until she came to the edge of the lake. The water glimmered darkly, its placid surface occasionally disturbed by a rising fish. As Ming-feng stood there she suddenly recalled the past. She remembered everything they had ever said or done together, she could visualise every tree, every blade of grass, so dear, so precious, knowing that she was leaving it all. The whole world was still. Everyone slept. Yet they were alive and would continue to live. She alone was going to die. . . .

Family concludes with Chüeh-hui's decision to leave the old life behind and go to Shanghai to take part in revolutionary activities. Romantically sentimental as writing like this may seem to a Western reader, it dealt with matters that were near the experience of many Chinese student readers. They easily identified themselves with the characters, and they were moved. In spite of sentimental excesses Pa Chin had a vivid poetic sense that made him the most widely read author among students before the Sino-Japanese War.

Lao She (see Plate 1) is the pen name of Shu Ch'ing-ch'un, born in 1897, and the first Peking writer to make his name in the new literary movement. His short stories and novels are marked by their humanism, clever type-characterisations, and skilful use of dialect. By dint of hard work and frugal living, Lao She took himself through the university, got a job and saved enough to go to London in 1929, where he taught Chinese at the London School of Oriental Studies and worked hard at his English. In his spare time he wrote a novel called *The Philosophy of Old Chang* which was accepted by *The Short Story Magazine* in Shanghai. Encouraged by this, Lao She began a long and successful literary career, which he nevertheless had to combine with academic work as the rewards of independent writing did not enable him to support his family.

During the war he worked hard for China's cause as the President of the All China Resistance to the Enemy Federation of Writers and Artists, an organisation with the kind of cumbersome title popular with the Chinese, which did useful work in fostering the arts under emergency conditions. Lao She first became associated with the theatre during the war and wrote several patriotic plays and ballads for recitation to musical accompaniment. In 1945 he was officially invited to the United States where he remained until 1949. His novel *Lo-t'o Hsiang-tzu*, better known in English as *Rickshaw Boy*, became a best seller in America in 1945, but Lao She objected to the happy ending tacked on by the translator, Evan King, which was not in the original text. Later he successfully sued King for the unauthorised publication of a second novel entitled *Divorce*. A new version by Helena Kuo called *The Quest for Love of Lao Lee* was later approved by Lao She.

Since returning to China in 1949, Lao She has remained active in an organisational capacity and as a writer of plays about social reform. But his reputation will rest on those early works which brought him fame by their accurate and sympathetic observation of Chinese life and character.

POETRY

Some of the greatest experiments of the new literary movement were in poetry. The Chinese had always treated poetry as a supreme form of artistic expression and had developed it to a point of technical perfection and elegance beyond which it seemed impossible to go. In their anxiety to overcome conformity the new poets went to extremes. They decided there was nothing to learn from a form that had outlived all its possibilities, and began to experiment with a wide range of Western forms from the sonnet to blank verse.

The very perfection of Chinese poetry made many of the new experiments seem the cruder. Some writers, for example, began by treating every Chinese character as an English syllable and produced a verse that was so monotonous in form and odd in content that it was nicknamed "beancurd" poetry by critics scornful of those who slavishly copied alien rhyming patterns. But in spite of all the freaks and failures a genuine vein of lyrical verse grew out of the new movement.

A significant event for new poetry was the founding of the New Moon Group in Peking. Its members had mostly studied in America. Their work was not immune from affectation, but as a whole it had considerable influence on the technical development of modern Chinese verse. Foremost among the group was Wen I-to (1899–1946), a scholar in several fields. Wen believed that while it was well enough for Chinese poets to adore the English sonnet, their admiration should not blind them to their own heritage as a source for new creation. As he put it: "If we refuse to admit there is beauty in new poetry using refined rhymes adapted from classical sources, we must then either choose between bad poetry or writing poetry in a foreign language."

Wen studied in America between 1922–35, both in

Chicago and Colorado. A visit to New York awakened his interest in modern drama and also brought him into contact with politically minded Chinese students there. A strong sense of nationalism awoke in him. There was a good deal of anti-Chinese feeling in the United States of the twenties, and this inspired Wen to write his famous poem, "The Laundry Song," expressing his agony of mind at the humiliation of his people. The first lines run:

> One piece, two pieces, three pieces.
> Washing must be clean.
> Four pieces, five pieces, six pieces.
> Ironing must be smooth.
> I can wash handkerchiefs wet with sad tears,
> I can wash shirts soiled with sinful crimes.
> The grease of greed, the dirt of desire,
> And all the filthy things in your house.
> Give them to me to wash, give them to me. . . .

On his return to China, Wen took up an academic career and did research on classical Chinese literature, a labour of love that occupied him until his death. Near the end of his life he was both saddened and angered by the national plight. He recanted criticisms he had once made about Lu Hsün, whom he now declared right for blaming China's troubles on intellectuals who remained aloof from national affairs. In September 1944, Wen joined the Democratic League, China's "Third Force," and edited their journal. Because of the Nationalist Government's brutal treatment of students who insisted on holding discussion meetings, Wen became more openly critical of official policy. As a result he was assassinated by government agents in July 1946.

Another important member of the New Moon Group was Hsü Chih-mo (1896–1931). Hsü studied in both America and England where he worked under Harold J. Laski for six months and met Katherine Mansfield, whose stories he later translated. Hsü was a charming and sociable person who on his return to China quickly became immersed in the literary-academic life of Peking, then a lively source of experiment and ideas. He was a pioneer in the movement to break away from tradition and create new and valid forms in poetry. He published four volumes of verse in his lifetime and though his work varied in quality, his love poems were rated among the best of their kind. His tragic death in an air crash cut short the career of a talented, sensitive artist and sophisticated individualist. In the last collection of verse published before his death Hsü wrote: ". . . a poet is like a mad bird. He presses his tender heart against the thorns of a white rose and sings the beauty of the moon and stars and the hopes of men. Not until the rose is dyed red from his heart's blood will he stop singing. Pain and happiness are one. . . ."

The role of Kuo Mo-jo in founding the Creation Society has been described earlier. Here a few words may be added about the distinctive place he holds as a poet. Kuo passed through a succession of influences during his career and each affected him with an equal intensity. Tagore was one of his first enthusiasms. The Indian poet achieved international fame in 1913 by winning the Nobel Prize and soon became popular in Japan where Kuo was a student. Kuo eagerly devoured everything of Tagore's he could lay his hands on. But by 1917–18 he was under the spell of Goethe whose *Faust* he translated and under whose influence he first experimented with play writing. In the autumn of 1919 he read Walt Whitman's *Leaves of Grass* and was profoundly moved by it. It was Whitman who first fired the spirit of rebellion in Kuo and inspired the fervent quality found in some of his earlier poetry, such as the opening lines of his "Earth My Mother" quoted below:

Earth, my mother,
The skies already brighten with the early dawn,
You arouse the child at your bosom
Now I clamber upon your back

Earth, my mother.
You sustain me as I wander through this paradise
And within the ocean you make music that comforts
  my soul.
Earth, my mother,
You are food, clothing and shelter to me
In the past, the present, and the future.
How can I repay your great kindness to me enough?
Earth, my mother. . . .

The love of bold imagery and exclamatory rhythm that was the raw material of Kuo's later revolutionary poems is already apparent in this excerpt.

There is space here for only two more poets, both belonging to a newer, politically concerned generation, Ai Ch'ing, born in 1916, and T'ien Chien, who first attracted attention by the poetry he wrote at Yenan, the Communist headquarters, during 1943.

Ai Ch'ing is, or rather was, before being purged, one of the more talented contemporary poets whose free-verse style has had a considerable influence on his generation. He spent his early childhood in the care of a peasant wet nurse in the Chekiang countryside, and the experience left a deep impression on his mind. Later it inspired one of his more powerful narrative poems epitomising the hard lot of the peasant. His passionate convictions led him to revolt against the existing authority, and in 1930, after a two-year stay in France, he was arrested and jailed in Shanghai by the French Concession police. The period of his confinement is uncertain, but during his imprisonment he wrote his first collection of poems, published in 1936. It included the poem inspired by the life of his old nurse that he called "an imprecation on an unjust world." In 1941 he arrived at Communist headquarters in Yenan, and his environment brought some political changes in his writing. When the Communists achieved power in 1949, Ai Ch'ing was still in favour, but in February 1958 he was expelled from professional and political life and like Ting Ling is now listed as a "bourgeois writer."

The Chinese landscape fascinated Ai Ch'ing and some of his most vivid imagery was created under its spell as in the following lines from his poem "Dead Land," on a drought in Szechuan:

75127

The land is dead.
The great desert that lies open
Is the corpse.
It died in despair
And while dying
Its parched eyes opened
Wishing that a drop of rain might fall
From the high heavens.
No rain.
Not a single drop of rain.
All we see everywhere are the scorched wheat stalks
That seem to have been burned
And the shrivelled wheat ears
And the dry cracked land. . . .

Or this impression from his poem "North":

. . . North China is a sad country
Sandstorms blow from the border
Taking away the green and the light of the sun.
Grey and yellow colours
Under a blanket of fog and dust. . . .

In his testament, *On Poetry*, written in 1940, Ai Ch'ing said: "The sound of poetry is the sound of freedom. Suppression of speech is the most cruel of any violence," an ironical avowal in view of what befell him.

T'ien Chien gave his early poems a drum-like metre, whose stark quality was much admired by Wen I-to in his last years. He named T'ien Chien "the drummer of our time" and called him a cleansing force in modern Chinese poetry. Just as all the complexities of melody had developed from the rhythmic monotones of the drum, Wen said, so too had poetry developed from the simple rhythmic lines. But development of technical method had too often been at the expense of feeling and this had weakened Chinese poetry a great deal. T'ien Chien's unpretentious style lacks romance or sentiment, it simply echoes the sound of battle or the cry of the peasant as in these lines from "More than A Hundred":

> They shout
> There on the sands where the blood is not yet dry
> The hearts of the farmers
> Marching
> A star on fire.

THE WAR PERIOD

The Sino-Japanese War period (1937–45), was characterised by technical re-appraisals of literature rather than by any creative contribution of lasting greatness. Propaganda and reportage were the order of the day. Typical of the period were plays and ballads written for performance in village squares. Designed to stir the public by their immediate emotional appeal, they dispensed with ambiguity or intellectual subtlety. Because cumulative and repetitive metres were needed, writers and poets fell back on the old folk ballads for their effects.

Wartime demands on writers hastened a development that had already been foreseen, a new standard of colloquial prose. By the late thirties the style developed after the May Fourth period had grown a little artificial, modernisation had begun to defeat the original purpose of direct communication. Chinese grammar is comparatively simple and generalised by Western standards, and sentences tend to be short and disconnected. In order to overcome this and bring a new continuity of thought and style into writing, modifying adverbs, relative clauses, and other types of Western literary construction had gradually been introduced. This helped to make translation of Western writing easier, but many writers and scholars began to feel the Chinese language had acquired so many mannerisms that there was a danger of usage being again divorced from living issues.

The war made writers face this problem. The mass shift of population to West China familiarised writers with the life and speech of people previously unknown to them. This and the need to arouse the patriotic feelings of ordinary people from so many different areas caused novelists, dramatists, and poets to discard artificial devices in favour of the simple direct speech of the everyday life around them.

The requirements of wartime propaganda eventually obscured the true nature of this movement, which gave some promise of a post-war renaissance. And political events since have turned it completely away from creative experiment towards Communist doctrinairism. The most significant wartime literary event—significant, that is, for the whole future of Chinese writing—was the meeting of cultural workers called at Yenan, in May 1942, when Mao Tse-tung made two speeches. The first raised a number of artistic and literary issues; the second summed up his conclusions and postulated the correct Party standpoint for artists and writers. Mao's pronouncements were immediately accepted as the cultural bible of the Communists to be reverently quoted in perpetuity.

Following the celebrated Yenan forum a great deal of writing and propaganda with no claims at all to being literature was poured out, but here and there were those who in following Mao's call produced something original. For example, Chao Shu-li, born to a Shansi peasant family in 1903, wrote with sincerity and directness about the life he knew. He had a great success in 1943 with *Hsiao Erh's Marriage,* a simple, sentimental village tale, followed by a second story, the *Rhymes of Li Yu-tsai,* in

31

which a village story-teller acting as *vox populi* helps to implement a new regime by his witty and earthy exposure of corruption and evil in the old society. Chao had an authentic peasant vocabulary and both these works were designed to be read aloud; the second one actually employed the rhyming technique of the professional story-teller. Chao's next work was more ambitious, a novel entitled *Changes in Li Village*, which described the events in a Shansi village from the war lord period in 1928 down to the defeat of the Japanese in 1945. His later work lacks something of his first freshness, as though he too has succumbed to the conformity that is the blight of modern Chinese writing.

THE CONTEMPORARY SCENE

By 1949 the Communists already commanded a great deal of support, both active and passive, from Chinese writers, and indeed from the bulk of Chinese artists. Practically everybody important in the arts attended the First National Conference of Writers and Artists at Peking in July 1949, after which the All China Federation of Literary and Art Circles was founded with a membership that covered every aspect of Chinese creative talent. But the literary output that has followed that auspicious occasion can only be described as dull in quality and content.

The old established writers have failed to produce any significant work under the Communist regime and many of them are silent altogether, or, like Ting Ling, have been silenced. The new writers are bound by the dead hand of conformity. Artists who wanted no part in the Nationalist regime, and whose creative talent in the past was nourished upon the historic social conflicts of the last fifty years, have been unable to continue their writing unless it has been completely subordinated to the class struggle, Party version. The spirit of the May Fourth Movement, the literary intellectual revolt, has been muzzled.

The writers' only allegiance is to the Party line, however inconsistent this may be from time to time. Politics dictate artistic theory, and when the official line has been promulgated the literary critic may disseminate the current jargon. Within such control there is little chance for writing to achieve anything but prosy artificiality.

The literary scene during the last ten years has been marked by several disputes and purges, accompanied by vicious public attacks on the persons concerned. The classic case is that of Hu Feng, the literary critic, whose name became the symbol of the Party's attack on bourgeois tendencies among intellectuals in 1955. The campaign to rid China of "Hu Feng deviationism" raged through the land for half a year. Hu Feng had been an associate of the famous Lu Hsün, closely connected with the leftist movement in literature, and a member of the Party though he never really supported its dictatorial control of art and literature. In 1954 to climax a series of disputes he wrote a long essay implying strong criticism of intellectual high-handedness by the Party. Like a pack of well-trained dogs on a cornered hare, the literary "faithful" rose and denounced him to a man. In July 1955 he was arrested, "tried," and vanished from the scene until June 1957 when he was released from jail during a new campaign of liberalisation.

What has become of the "old guard" of modern Chinese literature, many of whom have been discussed in this chapter? Kuo Mo-jo, that fiery intellect, is suitably embalmed as a figurehead, Chairman of the All China Federation of Artists and Writers, President of the Chinese Academy of Sciences, and Vice Chairman of the National Assembly, positions which carry high prestige but no actual power. Mao Tun, the once brilliant novelist, finds creative writing incompatible with his duties as Minister of Culture and official spokesman of the literary world. Lao She, most human of authors, manages to steer a professionally ambivalent course, but today writes only plays that pay nominal homage to social realism. Pa Chin, the idol of student readers, has done nothing except confess his lack of inspiration and write stereotyped reportage. Shen Ts'ungwen, robust chronicler of his own particular world, is granted literary recognition by having his name appear on a publication about traditional brocade designs. Ting Ling, *enfant terrible* of modern writing, has ended her career scrubbing floors. Ai Ch'ing, the poet, has been banished to outer silence with her. Lu Hsün alone has been elevated to the status of a literary god beyond whom there is only Mao Tse-tung. And Lu Hsün has long been dead.

With some of the most intelligent and creative authors in China dumb, it is not easy to know whether this is a matter of artistic conscience, self-interest, or plain survival, but it suggests that the writers themselves have no real faith in Marxist standards even though they propagate them to a younger generation unaccustomed to anything but the artificial inspiration of the Party muse. Of all artists in China the writer today is in the least enviable position. He can only wait for the process of awakening that must always follow a dragooning of the imagination. His worst fear is that the tempo may be too slow for his single lifetime.

III. THEATRE AND DANCE

The old-style Chinese theatre has remained a favourite with a majority of ordinary Chinese people. Even today it is a strongly entrenched and dearly loved art equalled in general popularity only by the cinema. In traditional Chinese drama the stage itself is bare, and every inch of it is utilised to gain a plasticity of effect. Time and space are dispensed with, and highly formalised techniques of gesture, speech, and mime are used to express the sharply differentiated personalities of the characters portrayed. The plays preach no sermons; right and wrong are directly contrasted on the basis of Confucian morality, particularly in the treatment of women whom this same morality required to be played by men on the stage. Until 1949 actors were trained to take women's roles. All through the nineteenth century and well into the first quarter of the twentieth it was considered immoral and unseemly for women to appear on the stage. Moreover, the widespread practice of foot-binding would have made it difficult for many of them to do so until after 1911 when foot-binding was finally abolished. In the old days the Chinese actor had to use a kind of miniature stilt on the stage to imitate the seductive gait of a coquette with bound feet, a practice that has now been discontinued.

The old theatre stood for many things the 1911 reformers opposed. Hu Shih himself argued for its relegation to the category of "useless survival," although this was an artistically unperceptive judgement at the time. In fact the new drama reformers could not dispense with the old theatre completely, and as they had no first-hand approach to good Western stage practice, and were often woefully ignorant of the true worth of their own theatre, it is not surprising that their first results were not outstanding as dramatic art, whatever they may have been as propaganda.

The history of the modern Chinese theatre begins in 1907. In that year a group of Chinese students in Tokyo, influenced by Japanese experiments with Western drama, formed the Spring Willow Society and staged their first play in February. It was called *Ch'a Hua Nü*, a Chinese version of Dumas' *La Dame aux camélias*, and was given in aid of a flood relief fund. The play had an all-male cast and used a strange mixture of old and new techniques, characteristic features of the "modern" drama for many years after that. It was the forerunner of a new style of drama called *hua-chü*, which literally means "speaking plays."

In June 1907, the Spring Willow Society staged *The Black Slave's Cry to God*, a five-act play based on a translation of Harriet Beecher Stowe's *Uncle Tom's Cabin*. The theme of protest against racial prejudice appealed to the nationalist feelings of Chinese students of the period, especially those in Tokyo, then the headquarters-in-exile of the new revolutionary party led by Sun Yat-sen.

The performance was imitated in Shanghai where a second Spring Willow Society was formed by Jen T'ien-chih and Wang Chung-sheng. They borrowed a theatre in the autumn of 1907 and for a month staged *The Black Slave's Cry to God*, to the great interest of Shanghai student society. Shanghai became an active centre of the new dramatic movement, especially in the schools. In May 1912, Li Chün-chiu and Chu Hsü-tung founded The Enlightenment Society (*K'ai-ming-she*), after which the new-style plays became nicknamed "enlightened drama" (*k'ai-ming hsi*). Another name used was "civilised drama" (*wen-ming hsi*).

The new theatre commanded attention as a political and

social propaganda medium in these early years, but no significant Chinese playwright appeared to develop it further, and production methods were rudimentary. A play would be prepared, often borrowing freely from other literary sources, and arranged in a number of scenes. It was then presented to the actors, who were relied upon to pull the story together on the stage. Although the substance of the dialogue was decided on beforehand, there was a good deal of improvisation. As Chinese audiences were unaccustomed to curtains or intervals, and considered themselves deprived of entertainment unless numbers were performed between the acts, this became a regular practice for every play staged. There was no production in our sense, and many of those taking part had never read a Western play much less seen one. In Shanghai any Western stage entertainment that went on was largely amateur and not available to Chinese.

The Western stage methods used in this period were mostly derived from Japan, but the actors still drew heavily on Chinese traditions for their technical interpretation. Although plots were intended to be realistic in their reflection of modern social conditions, the dialogue was often constructed on the speech rhythms and highly exaggerated effects of the old drama with its traditional musical accompaniment of brass and percussion. Above all, the strong prejudice against women appearing on the stage was not easily overcome, even in progressive revolutionary circles. It was not until the early twenties that actresses appeared in the modern theatre, and this was a retarding factor in its development. Though the "enlightened drama" was fairly popular for a time, it was at best only a half-baked imitation of Western theatre and produced a great deal of ham acting.

It also produced incongruities. In 1914, Mei Lan-fang (1894–1961), famous interpreter of women's roles on the classical Peking stage, appeared in a modern play called *The Waves of the Evil Sea*. It dealt with the question of prostitution, and at one point Mei appeared on the stage using traditional acting methods of speech and gesture but wearing a modern woman's dress and seated before a Singer sewing machine. Mei himself was keenly aware of new trends in the theatre world though he only dabbled on the fringe of the new-style dialogue drama.

In the years between 1912 and 1919, the new theatre made little real artistic headway, in contrast to the traditional drama which went from strength to strength, thanks to the example of Mei Lan-fang. During this period Mei became nationally acclaimed and added to his laurels by introducing a new series of plays into the classical repertoire. Called "ancient costume dramas," they were mostly dance pieces based on old choreographic forms long forgotten. They had an immediate success, and everyone flocked to see them.

Mei was assisted in preparing the plays for production by Ch'i Ju-shan (1876–   ), the first modern scholar to do practical research on the methods of the old theatre. The two men formed a partnership that lasted twenty years, and during this time Ch'i was the power behind Mei as playwright, adviser, and impresario. One of their greatest triumphs came when Mei was invited to take his troupe to the United States in 1930, the first time in history that Chinese drama had gone to the West.

On the eve of the now famous May Fourth outbreak in 1919, Mei was invited to perform in Tokyo, where he was greatly admired. He left China on April 21 and scored a great personal and artistic triumph. And on the momentous day when three thousand Peking students stormed the house of the Minister of Communications, and there as a political protest beat up China's Minister to Japan, Mei Lan-fang was preparing to perform his popular dance play *Heavenly Maiden Scattering Flowers* before a packed house in the Tokyo Kabukiza. It was a paradox of events.

After the May Fourth Movement there was a new attitude towards modern drama. A serious study of Western theatre began, and translations of such dramatists as Ibsen, Strindberg, Shaw, Wilde, Chekov, and Romain Rolland were made. New Chinese writers began to appear on the dramatic scene, one of whom, T'ien Han (1898–), was a true pioneer of the modern Chinese theatre. T'ien Han studied in Japan and was a member of the Creation Society, in whose journal his two plays *A Night at a Teahouse* and *Before Lunch* were first published and brought him recognition. He left the Society in 1925 to teach at a private, fine arts college, but soon started his own academy with a hundred of his former students, both men and women. The academy closed because of financial troubles, but out of it grew the South China Society (*Nan-kuo she*), a dramatic club which became a new theatre force under T'ien Han's leadership.

The South China Society gave their first Shanghai performance for three days in December 1928 when T'ien Han's own plays *Death of a Great Actor*, *The Will to Live*, *Drama at Sea*, and *Night Talk at Soochow* were staged. The first of these was about an actor who died on the stage for love of an actress who only then regretted her callousness. The second play concerned a father who drove his son from home when he learned the boy had had a love affair; but when his daughter revealed her illegitimate child, the sight of the baby softened his heart towards both his erring children. The third play was about a girl who refused to marry the man chosen by her parents. She pretended to commit suicide at sea and then haunted her parent's home as a "ghost." In this disguise she learned that the boy she loved was in fact already married, whereupon she really committed suicide. The last play dealt with a Peking professor who was separated from his family by civil war and as a refugee in the south finally discovered his daughter selling flowers.

Impossibly naive and sentimental as these plots sound, they provided some comment on social problems, especially relations between the sexes, but above all they were ready vehicles for experiments with new acting techniques. T'ien Han initiated a "small stage" movement intended to allow students to perform while studying and make some kind of living from it, however meagre (which it certainly was in those days). The South China Society travelled a circuit and gave performances in Soochow, Nanking, and Canton until the Nationalist authorities closed it down in 1930. In the following year T'ien Han became a member of the new Left-wing Dramatists League, a subsidiary of the League of Left-wing Writers. After that he became increasingly occupied in writing and producing plays with a revolutionary motive.

When the Japanese attacked Shanghai in 1932, the left-wing dramatists became too vocal for the liking of the Nationalist Government, who arrested several of the members, including T'ien Han. It was a period when a vicious government campaign was waged against writers and publishers with progressive ideas. Arrests were frequent, and many people lived in constant danger of being taken off. Seeds were laid then which bore bitter fruit in later years; the intellectuals never forgot.

Nevertheless, during the Sino-Japanese War T'ien Han worked for the Nationalist Government and held a high post in the Cultural and Propaganda Department. One of his tasks was the direction of touring Peking drama troupes in the Northwestern provinces, where they had a great success. He also experimented with revising and adapting several old plays, for which he was severely criticised by many who contended that he did nothing to improve the originals, although he had the co-operation of some famous actors. After the war he returned to Shanghai to teach but soon left for Hong Kong where he remained until 1948 when he joined the Communists in Manchuria. Today he is an important figurehead in literary-dramatic activities in Peking and has written some new historical costume plays.

T'ien Han is a significant figure in the early development of the modern Chinese drama. Although he has been a prolific writer, his plays, by Western standards, are loosely constructed, and exceedingly dull in their lack of dramatic tension. His greatest contribution has been in experimenting with and promoting new acting and production methods.

One of his associates in the South China Society, Ouyang Yü-ch'ien (1887–), merits a few words. He was an original member of the old Spring Willow Society in Tokyo, where he studied, and he has had a versatile career as playwright, film scriptwriter, actor, producer, teacher, and reformer. Moreover, he was active in both the traditional- and modern-style theatres. In his youth he was noted for his skilful playing of women's roles in the Peking style and was at one time compared favourably with Mei Lan-fang. In 1918 he was invited to direct an actors' training school in a model community founded by a well-known industrialist on the banks of the Yangtze River. The reforms in teaching and production of traditional drama that he carried out there were the forerunners of many technical changes made in the old theatre since 1949. During the twenties, as an actor on the modern stage, Ouyang Yü-ch'ien was to the fore in many developments. Besides collaborating with T'ien Han, he formed his own dramatic group in 1929, the Canton Dramatic Research Society. He finally gave up the stage, and in the thirties went to study film production in Europe and Russia. On his return he became well known as a scriptwriter in the Shanghai studios. His career covers modern Chinese theatre history in all its phases.

In November 1933, modern Chinese drama entered a new phase with the founding of the China Travelling Dramatic Troupe in Shanghai. This was a professional group which had a great success travelling round to play in different cities, thereby disproving the contention of those who held there was no audience to justify such an experiment with modern drama. The troupe had its greatest triumph in the spring of 1936 with the presentation in

Shanghai of *Thunderstorm*, a four-act tragedy by Ts'ao Yü, a youthful tyro who quickly leapt to fame as China's most successful dramatist in the Western genre.

Ts'ao Yü was born in Hupeh in 1910 and graduated from Peking University where he studied Western literature, particularly the plays of both classical and modern authors. His theatre interests had first been aroused as an actor-member of his school's dramatic club in Tientsin. *Thunderstorm* was published in a literary quarterly in 1934 and first staged in 1935 by the Fu-tan University Dramatic Club in Shanghai under the direction of Ou-yang Yü-ch'ien and Hung Shen (of whom more is said in Chapter IV). From Shanghai the play was taken on tour by the China Travelling Dramatic Troupe and played to record houses in every city it visited. *Thunderstorm* was banned three times by the Peking authorities of those days because it dealt with incest.

Thunderstorm is a long drama with prologue and epilogue. The action of the play, which takes place within twenty-four hours, is theatrically emphasised by the physical menace of a gathering storm. Using a wealthy industrialist's family to symbolise the disintegration of middle-class society, the plot describes the adultery of various members, whose spiritual destruction is revealed in clever dialogue and characterisation.

By Western standards the play is too long, has too little dramatic action, and contains stage devices that, to say the least, are a little timeworn. The prologue and epilogue of the original play were set in the waiting room of a Catholic hospital, and the curtain came down on this scene:

> Lu rises and stumbles a few steps towards the study until she reaches the centre of the stage where she slowly sinks down on her knees. The stage gradually darkens as the sound of Bach's Mass in B Minor, "Blessed is he that cometh in the name of the Lord," is heard. It starts faintly as though from a distance

and reaches a crescendo as the stage becomes completely dark, repeating the final action of the Prologue.

This is not the kind of material to make a Western critic enthuse on grounds of originality, and in all his work Ts'ao Yü relied heavily on what a Chinese writer called his "bag of tricks." He borrowed freely the ready-made devices of Ibsen and O'Neill. His play *Wilderness*, for example, written in 1936, was an obvious echo of *Emperor Jones*. His second play, *Sunrise*, written the previous year, also has derivative effects; the third act is set in a brothel and there is a reminiscent fondness for "putting everything in." But in spite of his borrowing Ts'ao Yü had a genuine sense of tragedy, possibly enriched by his early study of Greek drama, and at least he showed a technical soundness many of his predecessors lacked. He had a feeling for characterisation and a convincing knowledge of Chinese psychology that brought his plays alive for the receptive middle-class audiences then beginning to fill theatres now that the first crude pioneering experiments were over.

All Ts'ao Yü's best plays were written within six years. In addition to those already mentioned, there were *Metamorphosis*, written in 1940, *Peking Man*, in the same year, and *Family*, in 1941. Six in all, they represent the most powerful contribution of any single writer to the modern Chinese theatre. In 1946 Ts'ao Yü was invited to the United States on a cultural visit, but the trip had no productive effect on his writing after he returned to China. He was a presidium member of the First Conference of Chinese Writers and Artists held in Peking in July 1949, and from then until 1956 not a word came from his pen. In 1956 his new play, *Bright Skies*, was announced. The first performance was seen by the writer in Peking in May 1956. By any contemporary Western theatre standards it was an undistinguished performance. The plot concerns a dedicated bacteriologist on the staff of the former Peking Union Medical College who volunteers for the Korean front after becoming disillusioned by germ warfare. Chiefly anti-American propaganda, this dull play dashed any hope of a revival of Ts'ao Yü's former talent. His latest work was announced in 1961, a five-act historical play called *Gall and the Sword*. His former Freudian-type analysis of contemporary society is presumably being allowed no chances.

A playwright who had a considerable reputation in the nineteen-thirties is Hsia Yen, the pen name for Shen Tuan-hsien, born in Chekiang in 1900. He was prominent in left-wing literary circles and scored his first success as a dramatist with two plays, *Under Shanghai Roofs,* staged in 1935, and *Sai Chin Hua,* staged in 1936. The first depicted the bitter lot of tenement dwellers in Shanghai, and the second had for its subject a famous courtesan of Boxer Rebellion days. *Sai Chin Hua* caused quite a sensation and was widely discussed as a new way of using a historical theme to satirise society.

The period to which these two plays belong was a fruitful one for the modern Chinese theatre. The China Travelling Dramatic Troupe, which first put on Ts'ao Yü's plays, put a new spirit in stage activities and set the pace for the development of a professional modern theatre with an audience large enough to support and encourage it. In 1937 the Carlton Theatre in Shanghai was converted from a cinema into a regular arts theatre, a significant indication of the way the wind was blowing. This led to the formation of a professional group known as the Experimental Arts Theatre Company, which made its debut at the Carlton in June 1937 with a performance of *Romeo and Juliet* translated into Chinese. This had a mixed reception, but the succeeding production *Empress Wu Tse-t'ien,* a Chinese historical play by Sung Chih-ti, played to full houses. Hsia Yen's *Under Shanghai Roofs* and Ts'ao Yü's *Wilderness* were also put on by this group.

Other major theatre companies in Shanghai during this period were the Fourth Decade Company and the New South Company. In Nanking there were the Chinese Stage

Association, which in 1936 produced an adaptation of Tolstoy's *Resurrection* by T'ien Han, and The National Dramatic Academy, a government training school opened in September 1935 under the direction of Yü Shang-yuan (1897–   ), which began to stage monthly performances of modern theatre in January 1936. In Tientsin there was the Nankai University Dramatic Club, a veteran in the field of amateur production.

In 1937 a new Shanghai company, the Drama Workers Society, gave the first performance of Ts'ao Yü's *Sunrise*, winner of the *Ta Kung Pao* literary prize. The play, directed by Ou-yang Yü-ch'ien, was an immediate success. In the same year the leading dramatic groups in Shanghai staged a three-week joint performance to encourage wider support for the new theatre movement. Six plays were put on, *Thunderstorm* by Ts'ao Yü, *Spring Wind and Autumn Rain* by Ah Ying (pen name of Ch'ien Hsing-ts'un), Tolstoy's *Resurrection* adapted by T'ien Han, Somerset Maugham's *The Sacred Flame*, Chekov's *The Dog*, and Gogol's *The Marriage*, which had the greatest success of them all and was directed by Sung Chih-ti (1914–   ), an ardent patriot, revolutionary, and the son of a farmer.

In May 1937 a Union of Dramatic Groups was formed in Shanghai to make troupe co-operation easier and, not least, to strengthen the theatre movement by creating a patriotic united front against the growing threat of Japanese militarism. The construction of a new arts theatre, The Twentieth Century, was planned, with a formal opening scheduled for October and a new company directed by Sung Chih-ti. But by that time China was involved in a bitter struggle, and Sung had collaborated with other dramatists to produce *The Marco Polo Bridge*, a propaganda play based on the incident that had precipitated full-scale war and marked the end of an era in the arts for China.

The open aggression of the Japanese in 1937 released a pent-up flood of Chinese hatred which was vehemently expressed on the stage. Touring troupes were organised everywhere, and actors travelled the country performing in villages, factories, and before the troops. The theatre entered a new phase of popularity; Chungking and Chengtu became lively dramatic centres in the Nationalist area. Besides the playwrights already mentioned, there were several others who had a wartime vogue. One was Ch'en Pai-ch'en (1907–   ), an early member of T'ien Han's South China Society, and the organiser in 1937 of the Shanghai Stars Troupe, which travelled round West China staging propaganda shows. Ch'en's *Autumn Fields,* which described the co-operation of the army and the farmers, was listed as one of the ten best representative plays of the war.

Another wartime figure was Hsiung Fo-hsi (1900–   ), a graduate of Columbia University, who between 1932 and 1936 directed a rural theatre in Hopei under the auspices of the National Association for Mass Education Movement. During the war he led his troupe, The Farmers' Enemy Resistance Dramatic Corps, to Chengtu where they performed before audiences numbering thousands. Several of Hsiung's own plays were staged. Ting Hsi-lin (1893–   ), a British-trained physicist, who had been known for his witty comedies, wrote several plays which were very popular in wartime Chungking, and his one-act plays were widely staged in the schools. Lao She, the novelist, also began to write patriotic plays during this period, and since then has remained constantly faithful to the theatre.

In spite of this varied talent and public enthusiasm, the wartime theatre was not able to sustain the rate of artistic progress made in pre-1937 years. It was too closely shackled by the demands of propaganda and patriotic sentiment, which created an artistic vacuum with no escape for the playwright who had something personal to say. In the Communist guerilla areas the theatre became a political medium of another kind, and a method for educating the peasant to a correct understanding of the proletarian struggle according to Marxist interpretation. To achieve this, and following the famous 1942 Yenan forum, great attention was given to dramatic techniques based on folk dancing and ballad singing with themes emphasising peasant life and activity.

In 1944, the Lu Hsün Art Academy at Yenan produced a play called *The White-Haired Girl* which has become a landmark in Communist theatre history. It was based on a Hopei legend discovered by Communist cadres in 1938, and it had been a popular theme of the rural story-tellers before it arrived at Yenan and was transformed into a stage entertainment. The legend tells of a peasant girl whose father is forced to sell her as a concubine to pay his debts to the local landlord. The old man commits suicide in shame, and in spite of her true love's efforts to save her, the girl is dragged off and deflowered. After tiring of his victim, the evil landlord plans to kill her, but she escapes to the mountains where she lives in a cave and gives birth to a child. As the result of her sufferings her hair turns completely white, and peasants who catch glimpses of her from time to time think she is a spirit and make offerings to her in the local temple. In the Communist version, she is eventually found by Communist cadres to whom she tells her true story. *The White-Haired Girl*, which was also made into an opera in 1945, and revised in 1949, is an artistic symbol of the period in which the Communists came to power.

THE CONTEMPORARY SCENE

Since 1949 the theatre has passed through many political phases, but the Communists have not been slow to realise the value of a well-run subsidised theatre. When they arrived in Peking in 1949 they immediately put a temporary ban on fifty-five plays belonging to the old theatre repertoire. The reasons given were that they encouraged superstitious beliefs, were licentious, or depicted the defamation of the Chinese race at the hands of foreign invaders. Among the latter was the famous and exceedingly popular play *Ssu Lang Visits His Mother*, an old favourite of amateur actors. It was finally restored to favour again in May 1956 with a performance, seen by the writer, in the Chung Shan Park in Peking before an audience of more than three thousand.

From 1949 to 1953, the traditional forms of Chinese art were generally played down in high political quarters, and it was not until the Second Congress of Chinese Literary and Art Workers in October 1953 that Kuo Mo-jo pronounced an official blessing which heralded their return to grace. Some months before this the Institute of Dramatic Research in Peking issued an official break-down of the position of the traditional theatre repertoire. Sixty-three plays were listed as rearranged, fifteen as being new or drastically revised, while more than two hundred continued to be staged as before, which says something for the resilience of the old theatre during some of its most difficult days.

The banning or changing of old plays has been a favourite weapon of attack on Communist cultural policy from the outside. Without in any way condoning doctrinaire reforms it might be pointed out that the banning of plays for political purposes is not a Communist prerogative. Although the technique is practised on a larger scale now, it was also common in Ch'ing and Republican days. Apart from this, many Chinese plays have no rigid version and have been subject to the individual actor's revisions in the past. And since scores of traditional plays take as their theme the struggles of ordinary people against corrupt officials and despotic authority, it has not been necessary for the Communists to change what was already on the stage but only to slant it.

In spite of the fact that the Marxists have constantly poked their fingers into the theatre pie during the last ten years, a considerable part of the old repertoire flourishes as vigorously as ever. Among the Chinese it is said that

Chou En-lai has been the saviour of the old theatre, which he admires. He was a talented amateur in his youth and played women's roles; he was also friendly with Mei Lan-fang and visited the great actor in hospital before he died. Whatever the real facts about Chou's reputed championship of the old drama, no one can deny that it is very much alive today.

State control of the Chinese theatre is heavily criticised in some outside circles today, although it is difficult to see how any other measure could have rescued the stage from the bankrupt state it was in before 1949. The Chinese theatre as an entity has been saved by State intervention, and the general standards of training and technical resources have been improved. State subsidy allows traditional troupes to be run as permanent working units, and this is important in a theatre whose personnel requirements resemble those of Western ballet companies. There is a much higher general level of technical proficiency among the rank and file of traditional troupes today, while the ill-disciplined audiences and badly kept auditoriums of pre-1949 days have gone, and no one with any love for the theatre can regret the fact.

Within recent years there has been an active trend to revive local dramatic forms throughout the country. Implicit in this is a political motive, because these forms are regarded as unsophisticated versions of theatre art, true "people's entertainment." Be that as it may, a wealth of interesting stage material has been re-discovered in the process. A typical example of what is being done is provided by the Soochow drama, *The Fifteen Strings of Cash*, an old favourite of last century, revived in 1956 (see Plate 3). It is true that the new version has been revised, but merely in the sense that in its old form it would have been tediously long for contemporary audiences, who are not the dedicated connoisseurs their forefathers were. The revisions have been made in the cause of practical working theatre and nothing more sinister than that.

When the writer first saw the play in 1956, it had created a furore, and a good deal of party ink was being spilt one way and the other because the play was hailed as a successful example of official cultural policy to "weed through the old and let the new emerge." The fact remains it was an excellent piece of dramatic entertainment which retained the true spirit of Chinese theatre. The story is about a young couple wrongly condemned to death by a stupid magistrate on the charge of murdering the girl's stepfather, a drunken old pork butcher, and eloping with his cash. A more perceptive junior magistrate by a smart piece of detective work pins the crime on the real culprit, Lou the Rat, gambler, rogue philosopher, and murderer through circumstance, a role played by a comic actor who is more than a mere farceur. The mime and expression of the old-style actor who played the part in 1956 constituted one of the great performances of the Chinese stage, reminiscent of Marcel Marceau in the West.

There have been considerable technical changes in staging, lighting, and production within the limits of the proscenium-style stage which is now universal in China. Even the old drama, which at the beginning of the century still had its audience seated on three sides of a square platform stage, today uses the Western proscenium form with a main curtain plus two more, enabling the stage to be partitioned for scene changes. This may seem a little ironical at a time when the Western theatre is eagerly exploring the dramatic possibilities of the open stage, but Chinese ingenuity in using methods new to China cannot be denied. The orchestra and the property men are no longer visible to the audience as in the past. The myriad sightseers who used to crowd the stage wings of the old Chinese theatre, to the detriment of good play viewing, have been sent back where they belong—to the auditorium —and the efficiency and dignity of the performance are the better for it.

In the new Western-style theatre there are technical resources and trained personnel on a scale hitherto unknown in China. But the playwrights are still groping, and political conformity keeps their work parochial in its approach. Apart from this, there remains the fact that China has not yet produced a playwright whose work can be ranked with the great Russian or Western masters.

Students of the Western-type theatre now take a four-year course at the Central Dramatic Institute opened in Peking in 1950, a merger of the old National Dramatic Academy from Nanking with certain university drama sections. Students may specialise in acting, stage production, or designing. Russian advisers are attached to the school, and Stanislavsky methods have been emphasised. After graduation, the students, mostly of university age, are posted to numerous professional troupes that draw upon the school for personnel. The old apprentice system has been abolished in the traditional theatre—it had more or less disappeared before 1949 in any case—and pupils enter the Peking Drama School at the age of eleven for a minimum seven years of training that includes general education and political instruction. Boys are no longer taught women's roles, although many of the old-time female impersonators are still active, chiefly as instructors of the new generation of actresses. The Peking Drama School was opened in 1952, and its first group of graduates, sixty-five in all, made their professional debut in July 1959. Each of them had learned about sixty different plays before being assigned to one of the leading Peking troupes to begin their stage careers.

The Chinese theatre in general is still in a process of transition. It is a mixture of old and new forms which have not yet reached a harmonious meeting. From an international point of view, it is in the fields of less realistic stage art, mimetic techniques, and dance drama, that the Chinese are best equipped to make a contribution to stage art beyond their own boundaries. And the Communists are very sensibly ensuring that the traditional genre is preserved as a necessary basis for a national theatre. Although the right creative synthesis for a contemporary theatre has not yet been discovered there can be no doubt of the tremendous potentialities being engendered.

THE DANCE

The dance has a long history in China, as both ritual and Court entertainment, but by the time of the Revolution in 1911 it had become a neglected art in any public sense. True, there were the festival dances of the rural areas, the dance rites of Confucian temples, and in the old theatre there was a vocabulary of stylised movement which was dancing in its basic sense. But these forms were distinct and apart and in the last two cases used only male performers.

By the late nineteen-twenties the situation had radically changed, at least in the large cities where Western style education for women was proceeding apace. Eurythmics, Russian ballet, and the American chorus line all had their devotees, while ballroom dancing had arrived to stay. The sing-song girl of tradition rapidly yielded pride of place to the taxi dancer as jazz and the fox trot caught on among the more sophisticated younger Chinese in town society. A Hong Kong dance instructor said in 1922: "The craze for dancing has touched even the Chinese. Many of them are to be seen now in our ballrooms, whereas a few years ago it was something unthinkable to them. I have many pupils among them and they make good dancers . . . supple, graceful, and too conservative for any bizarre effects."

Shanghai naturally became the centre of the dance craze, and taxi dancers were an important feature of the notorious night life of that city. A press report of 1937 provided a new angle on their profession. "Patrons who dance with their wives are looked on with great disfavour by managements and dancers alike," it ran. "To avoid friction a new custom is in the making. The wife accompanies her husband on his dancing expeditions but sits out on the sidelines while he takes his turn with the beautiful professional partners. The system works well. The girls get their full share of business, and the wife remains serene in the knowledge that her husband is properly chaperoned. Many Chinese wives have not learned to dance, yet enjoy jazz music . . . some even bring their books or knitting. . . ."

The Shanghai wives were more tolerant than the Nationalist Government, for whom ballroom dancing remained a thorn in the flesh. There were constant attempts to put it down. In Nanking in 1937 when the guardians of Chiang Kai-shek's New Life Movement thundered that the capital must be kept morally clean, a ban on public dancing was imposed by the mayor, and in Shanghai the tax bureau was ordered to increase pressure on the dance profession. Campaigns like this continued sporadically through the years, but it took the Communists to banish ballroom dancing completely.

There were more "respectable" forms of dancing in the twenties and thirties. Many of the big girls' schools in Shanghai, Tientsin, and Peking, including several run by missionaries, had dancing on their curricula as part of physical training. Folk dancing displays in the Western manner were staged, Grecian rhythms and other kinds of movement to music were in vogue. The girls of the Shanghai Tungnan Physical Training School in 1934 appeared wearing blouses, shorts, and ankle socks, as they emulated the leg prancings of the Broadway chorus girl (see Plate 4). Shanghai also had its ballet lessons; there were several teachers among the large White Russian colony there. One was George Goncharoff, with whom Margot Fonteyn had her first instruction; no Chinese student attained her calibre.

All this activity created a receptive atmosphere, particularly towards the freedom of women to participate, but it could scarcely be called a national dance movement. Chinese dancing proper was seen only on the stage where the actor Mei Lan-fang did a great deal to popularise classical styles. Tribal dances were still preserved in many areas, and sporadic attempts were made to adapt a few of these as folk dances, but there was no systematic study or research that produced practical results. Until the war years, and apart from the theatre, China had nothing to show in the way of a dance movement.

In 1942 a new star appeared on the horizon, Tai Ai-lien, destined to become the leading spirit in a national dance renaissance. Tai Ai-lien was born in 1916 in Trinidad, West Indies, and as a child showed great dancing talent. In 1931 she went to England to study at the Jooss School of Ballet at Dartington Hall in Devon. She worked under Anton Dolin and Marie Rambert and gained some film and stage experience, but her heart lay elsewhere and in 1940 she left England for China, via Hong Kong, to study Chinese folk dances. On her arrival in China she taught and performed in wartime Chungking where she formed her own troupe, the Chinese Ballet Group, with the pupils who had gathered around her. They spent a great deal of time travelling in different areas, Tibet and Sinkiang especially, studying local dance techniques and adapting them for stage performance. Tai Ai-lien soon had a national reputation as a dancer-choreographer with a contribution of her own to make. By the end of the war she had laid a sound foundation for the development of a national dance tradition.

In 1946 she accompanied her husband, Yeh Ch'ien-yü, the artist, whom she had married in Chungking, to the United States and gave several dance recitals there. After her return in 1947 she reportedly separated from Yeh and did some teaching in Shanghai before going to Peking. There she carried on her ambition to promote the study and performance of the dance, a task in which she was given active encouragement by the Communist Government after 1949. In that year the whole of China ushered in the new regime by doing the *yang-ko*, a simple, peasant rice-planting dance that became the Carmagnole of the Chinese Communist Revolution. In every town and city, students and school children paraded the streets, advancing, retreating, side-stepping in long files winding in and out to the insistent da, da-da-da, da-da, da-da-da of the waist drum. For a time the *yang-ko* and its derivative forms superseded every other form of dancing. But as the first revolutionary fervour subsided the *yang-ko* gave way before the first phase of what has become a tremendous revival of traditional dancing in which Tai Ai-lien has been a dominant personality.

In 1953 prior to her appointment as principal of the Peking Dance School she made an extensive tour with two musicians, studying and recording the dances of various provincial areas. The school, founded in 1954, was the first establishment of its kind in China. Curriculum and training were organised with the help of Russian advisers. By 1955 the enrolment was given as 180 students with forty instructors. Today there are five times that number of teachers and more than three hundred students. Selection is very strict, and pupils are taken between the ages of eleven and fourteen for a seven-year course in which traditional Chinese choreography is the basic study, although the rudiments of Western ballet dancing are also taught. Great attention is given to studying the dances of the various autonomous tribal areas in China as well as those of other Asian countries. Emphasis has been laid on building up a national repertoire drawn from these sources. The Peking school has been a very successful experiment, and since its founding has put a number of talented troupes on the road. It is now being followed by counterparts in other cities.

Like Communists everywhere, the Chinese are dominated by the term "folk art," refusing to admit that dancing adapted for sophisticated urban stage presentation is hardly the same thing. Not that such adaptations are necessarily artistically bad; the Japanese theatre, for example, provides an example of how well this kind of thing can be done. And although some of the new dance experiments in China are marred by sentimentality or over-emphasis on realism, the general level of achievement of the new dance movement is nevertheless impressive, and a sound basis of technical proficiency has been created. On a more ambitious scale there have been several full-scale dance-dramas which exploit the acrobatic techniques of the traditional stage.

In December 1959 the Peking Dance School set up an experimental ballet troupe. The first full-length productions attempted were *Swan Lake* and Adam's *The Corsair*, directed by the Russian adviser to the school, P. A. Gusev. A new ballet, *The Maid of the Sea*, based on traditional Chinese dance forms was also staged. What the Chinese will eventually make of Western ballet remains open to conjecture. They themselves are the first to admit they are in the early stages of instruction and experiment. In the Russians they at least have the masters of a creative tradition to guide them.

During recent years Chinese theatrical troupes have travelled extensively in Europe, Canada, South America, and practically every major Asian country. The general climate of opinion wherever they have gone has been one of appreciation for their verve, precision, and stage appeal. In every case a dance group has been a part of each theatrical troupe, and dance performances are now a regular feature of repertoire. These international performances mark a new era in the old Chinese theatre. To decry them simply on the grounds of "cultural propaganda" is to deny the visible evidence of a great dramatic tradition resurgent.

THE PUPPET THEATRE

One pleasing aspect of the theatrical scene in contemporary China has been the revival of the puppet theatre. The Chinese puppet show has a long history; shadow puppets are mentioned in chronicles of the Sung dynasty (960–1278 A.D.). A favourite legend credits the invention of the shadow play to a Court necromancer of 121 B.C., who attempted to console the Emperor Wu of the Han dynasty for the loss of a favourite concubine by recalling her "spirit" with the aid of a puppet made in her image. Less romantic sources ascribe the puppet's origin to early religious observances.

Over a long period of time the different provinces have produced their own characteristic puppet forms. In addition to the famous shadow puppets of Peking and West China, there are both marionettes (string puppets) and hand-manipulated puppets. Fukien is noted for both styles; the Chuanchow marionettes, for example, are famous of their kind and remarkable for the complicated evolutions they can perform. The hand puppets of Canton are distinguished by their size—they are between three and four feet high—and the beautiful carving of their wooden heads.

But of all Chinese forms, the Peking shadow puppets have probably the greatest international renown. They are silhouette cut-outs made from donkey skin tanned to the transparency of glass and coloured. The arms, legs, and hands are articulated and the heads are detachable, enabling them to be used in a variety of costumes. The puppet is manipulated by three wires attached to each hand and the neck in order to keep the figure pressed flat against the screen on which the silhouette is projected. The puppets are manipulated behind a screen that was formerly made of paper, then of cloth, and is now made from opaque glass lit by fluorescent light. In the older style, the electric bulb is suspended about two feet from the rear of the screen at the centre.

These small figures about a foot high bear a remarkable resemblance to life as they cavort about their little world. The puppeteers are accompanied by musicians who use the same instruments as those found on the traditional Peking stage, from which many of the shadow plays are taken. The musicians also vocalise for the shadows when supernatural cries, battle slogans, and so on are required, and the parts for the roles are sung just as in the theatre of human actors. All the old favourites of the Peking stage repertoire are performed, although the puppet man has always been at liberty to improvise and adapt his own bits of "business," jokes, and satire according to his needs. Often no two performances are exactly the same and this gives the shadow plays an added attraction. In the old days the shadow theatre was an entertainment that travelled round performing at various family festivals—weddings and the like. In the Ch'ing period the shadow play was a favourite form of entertainment for the Palace women who were secluded from the outer world and its events.

The social changes of Republican China and the many new entertainments that developed in consequence caused a steady waning in the popularity of the puppet show in all parts of the country, and the shadow theatre of Peking was hard hit. In the years just following the 1911 Revolution, Peking was recorded as having thirty shadow troupes. By 1948 there was only one company left. The writer recalls visiting their workshop in 1947 when they were already more or less immobilised except when called out for an occasional show by some curious foreign household. Early in 1948 the American cultural authorities in Nanking presented an extensive collection of shadow puppets and their props to the Chinese National Museum, a generous contribution which seemed, however, at the time to symbolise the end of an active shadow theatre.

Today the puppets are once more dancing. As the result of a great revival, they are no longer museum pieces and are performing on a scale that has been unknown for many a year. The Communists took a speedy hand in searching out the old puppeteers and their troupes in every province, and in 1953 a programme of sponsorship was set up under the Ministry of Culture. A National Puppet Theatre was started under the auspices of the Ministry in Peking, and

Sergei Obraztsov, the famous Russian puppeteer, was invited to China as an adviser and consultant. In January 1954 a national puppet festival was organised, and troupes from eight different provinces took part during a session lasting eight days. Nearly forty different plays were staged, each representative of the style of its particular area.

Since that date the puppet theatre has consolidated its strength and several troupes have toured abroad in both East and West Europe. In June 1957 Paris saw its first performance of a Chinese puppet show, using both shadow puppets and marionettes, at the Théâtre Marigny.

The traditional repertoire of folk tales and legends is in full swing once again, but, as was to be expected, many new plays have been added. The first selection of these was seen at a nineteen-day festival organised by the Ministry of Culture in Peking and given by the leading provincial troupes. Among the old favourites performed by the shadow troupes on this occasion were *The White Snake* and *Pilgrimage to the West,* featuring the Monkey King, as formidable a character on the shadow screen as on the stage. And in addition to old-timers like these there were fifty new plays on contemporary themes, indicating that, like everyone else, the puppet was expected to do his share of proselytising.

A typical example was *Battling the Waves on the Lotus River at Night,* which opened with a theme song: "Swiftly we sail our sampans up the river, row, row, row . . ." and then, as a commentator described it, when the song ends a panorama of the rolling Lotus River is revealed with an endless file of heavily loaded sampans. It is 1958, at the height of the drive for more iron and steel. Four enterprising girls come to borrow a sampan from old Uncle Pao, the boat keeper. He agrees to lend them one but doubts their ability to get it across the rapids and advises male assistance. In the end he helps the girls to deliver their load of charcoal for the furnaces himself. On the way he dozes off at the tiller and the girls tickle his nose amidst shrieks of laughter, the incident providing an opportunity for many grotesque antics on the screen. Eventually the boat enters smoother waters and the girls proudly want to know if Uncle Pao still thinks boys are better than girls. Of course Uncle Pao has only one answer. The narrative continues, "The East shines red and their destination, the iron works, appears on the horizon." Encouraging the girls to a final effort, Uncle Pao steers the craft on a last spurt, accompanied by an old boatman's song set to new words:

> Yoho, yoho,
> We are heroes made of steel;
> No shoals or rapids can daunt us girls,
> United we are strong,
> The sky glows red beneath the glorious sun.

So much for the puppet in its new role of propagandist for steel production and equality for women. According to an official spokesman, "Shadow and puppet-theatre workers have successfully infused new ideas into the ancient arts, raising the traditional pieces to a higher level of artistry and producing modern plays of distinction with an effective treatment of contemporary socialist themes." But how long many of these new productions will survive must be a matter of some opinion. The most important thing seems to be that the puppet theatre as a dramatic form has been rescued from oblivion.

THE STORY-TELLER

Story-telling and balladry are two of the world's oldest forms of entertainment, and in China they have persisted with an astonishing vigour through the centuries. During wars and revolutions the story-teller has continued his craft and he is as popular as ever today. The radio has given him larger audiences, and his work has been granted enthusiastic recognition under the Chinese Communist regime as both a true "people's art" and a useful means of spreading the new social gospel.

The story-teller, like every other artist, is expected to do his bit for politics. He is more fortunate than some in that he can sometimes get away with criticising certain aspects of the bureaucratic scene through his humour and wit. As long as he does not attack the great ones and their policies he can occasionally get in some sly digs. This is not a new state of affairs in his history, and the story-teller is a past master at the *double entendre*. In subjects that are too obvious to be healthy he can always resort to historical allusion, and none understand that better than the Chinese.

The story-tellers and ballad-singers of the cities have always performed in special houses or small theatres, while in the country districts they strolled from village to village, performing in the local teahouse or setting up a pitch in the town square. Today they work a more organised routine, for they are sent to do their share of entertaining in factories and communes. As in the other dramatic arts, story-telling festivals are held from time to time in Peking, and performers from various provincial areas come to demonstrate their art and to show off the new pieces in their repertoires as well as the old favourites.

In the old days story-telling was often a leisurely business, and a performer would continue his narrative over a week or two, stopping at the critical juncture each day to make sure of his audience on the morrow. This was good business, but the pace of modern times, at any rate in the cities, meant that the story-teller had to speed things up a little, and it has been customary in recent times to relate the masterpieces from the old romantic novels in individual episodes that can be narrated separately or in sequence as an integrated story. But besides the lengthy tales from the past, the repertoire is full of short sketches and comic turns which it has always been the story-teller's business to keep up to date and salted with contemporary wit and allusions. Today, for obvious reasons, there have been extensive additions to the general repertoire and the wise cracks tend to refer repetitively to the evil past and the wonderful present. But a great deal of the old material continues to be performed, and the story-tellers undoubtedly have a status they never had before.

Story-telling and balladry are considered the "small arts" by the Chinese, and, as with the theatre, there are almost as many different styles as there are localities in China. The Yangtze valley area around Nanking, Shanghai, and Soochow has always been a happy hunting ground for the story-teller. In Shanghai the "small artists" command as large a following as any of the popular actors in the large theatres.

Story-tellers and ballad-singers number both men and women among their ranks, and a team often consists of two members of opposite sex. Some of the most distinguished performers are women. Traditional attire is the Chinese gown for both men and women, and if they do not accompany themselves with a musical instrument their only other accessories are a fan or handkerchief and a vocabulary of gestures which bring a galaxy of characters to life through the narrator's powers of suggestion.

The techniques of the story-teller's art range through many styles, with or without musical accompaniment. A popular form is *ta-ku-shu*, in which the narrator performs to the rhythmic beats of a small drum and a pair of hardwood clappers to emphasise the tempo and climaxes of such pieces as the old tales from the *Three Kingdoms* saga or stirring legends from the novel *Shui Hu Chuan*, known in English as *All Men Are Brothers*.

P'ing-hua is a form of story-telling in which no musical instruments are used. It is a highly developed art in the Soochow area, where the performers are noted for their extremely skilful sense of characterisation. The story-teller not only describes the situation and surroundings in his tale but portrays the characters concerned and at the same time records their thoughts and reactions for the benefit of his audience. A favourite method is to dwell on one small incident—perhaps a woman anxiously awaiting the arrival of her lover—which can become the starting point for a pattern of subtle and extremely expressive gestures in which the wave of a hand or the rolling of the eyes indicate a whole wealth of human emotions. Occasionally the Soochow story-tellers use song to heighten dramatic effect. A solo performance in which there is no musical accompaniment and the effect is entirely dependent on the narrator's vocal skill, facial expression, and hand gestures, is probably as superb a demonstration of the art of knowing what to leave out as may be seen anywhere. Needless to say, the best performers spend a lifetime mastering their clever craft.

Another kind of solo performer accompanies his narration with a *san-hsien*, a three-stringed, long-necked instrument which was the progenitor of the Japanese *samisen*. Performing with this instrument is known as *t'an-tz'u*. Sometimes there are two performers, usually a man and a woman, one of whom plays the *san-hsien* and the other the *p'i-p'a*, or pear-shaped lute. Or, very often, a man takes a woman's role in these performances. Such a team may, for example, impersonate a mistress and her maid.

Humour naturally is the essence of the story-teller's art, and well-timed flashes of wit driven cunningly home are eagerly savoured by the audience. Technically termed the "jewels" of a performance, they range between direct satire and gentle insinuation, but whatever form it takes the humour of the story-teller has a character of its own that once heard, and seen, is never forgotten. And this may be said to constitute the epitome of the good story-teller. He aims not just to win the immediate laugh but get below the skin so that his hearers chuckle whenever they recall the particular moment.

63

The *hsiang-sheng* is a purely comic turn, which may be a monologue or dialogue with one or two comedians engaged in a rapid fire of comic narration and repartee. Even when it is a single performer, he may enact two people until the audience is in roars of laughter listening to him answering himself back or taking both sides in an argument.

The Shanghai story-tellers have recently become very popular in Peking, where they performed at one of the festivals that since 1958 have become a regular feature of the cultural scene. The favourite entertainers of the common people have acquired a new lustre and a new repertoire simultaneously. The deeds of revolutionary heroes, the achievements of industrial production, and the beneficence of Chairman Mao, now find a place among age-old tales of great warriors, Imperial concubines, and courageous tiger hunters. In the words of one enthusiastic Communist critic, the old story-tellers, "finding the current activities throughout the country an inexhaustible source of inspiration," have added many new items to their repertoire, like "First Spring of the Sixties," which reflects the "spirit of the great leap forward." Great leaps notwithstanding, the story-teller will no doubt find a way to go round. He is irrepressible.

IV. THE CINEMA

The Chinese were early film fans. Charlie Chaplin and the other old silent stars had their following in China as in the West. But it was not until the early twenties that the Chinese began to make their own films, and even then by Western standards their production was small and technically inferior. The Chinese commercial market remained dominated by Hollywood movies until the late thirties.

The cinematograph first arrived in Hong Kong at a time when there was a mounting enthusiasm for the new entertainment in America and Europe. In October 1902 an article appeared in *The Hongkong Telegraph* describing how "The Twentieth Century Projectoscope Company, armed with Edison's latest invention" had given an interesting performance at the City Hall. Unfortunately an "incompetent substitute" had replaced a sick operator and there were "several hitches during the display." But in spite of this bad start, the cinema had come to stay. By 1907 the local press carried regular advertisements like this one: "Star Cinematograph, Wyndham Street. Every night commencing 6 P.M. Continuous performance. We never repeat our pictures."

From Hong Kong the invention quickly reached Shanghai, where in 1903 we hear of Señor A. Ramos, a Spaniard, renting the ground floor of the Ch'ing Lien Ko teahouse to present five o'clock cinematograph performances for a five-copper cash entrance fee (about fifty cents by present-day standards). His enterprise prospered, and the Señor went into business on a larger scale as the Ramos Amusement Company.

In the same year there are records of a Chinese called Lin Chu-san renting the T'ien Lo teahouse in Peking to show European and American films. And in his memoirs the actor Mei Lan-fang describes a film featuring the stage veteran T'an Hsin-p'ei being made out of doors in Peking in 1908. For all this early Chinese interest, Westerners were the first to attempt large-scale film making in China, and many of *their* attempts were rudimentary.

In 1909 an American named Brosky founded the Asian Motion Picture Company in Shanghai and produced two films *The Empress Dowager* and *The Unfortunate Child,* a prophetic title as it turned out for the venture failed. According to an obituary notice in the *North China Daily News* in 1937 a Neapolitan named Enrico Lauro was making films in China as early as 1905. After shooting a film on tea culture, he was reported to have attempted a feature entitled *The Curse of Opium.* He used boys for the women's roles, but they apparently committed every known beginner's crime and stared the camera out of countenance. After four months' unequal struggle Lauro consigned *The Curse of Opium* to oblivion. He was also said to have made documentaries of the Empress Dowager's funeral and the first flying exhibition by the French aviator Vallon over Shanghai in 1911.

A second American businessman tried his hand at film making in Shanghai in 1913 when he founded the Hsin Min Motion Picture Company. His partners were Chang Shih-ch'uan and Cheng Cheng-ch'iu who belonged to the "modern" theatre and were pioneer film actors. They made *Breaking Open the Coffin,* based on a traditional Peking play, and *A Wronged Ghost in the Underworld.* Both pictures were a hotch-potch of old stage techniques in which actors played women's roles, and their only exhibitor was the Y.M.C.A.

The Chinese themselves usually start their film history in 1917 when Pao Ch'ing-hua of the Commercial Press in Shanghai bought up the equipment of yet another

American optimist who had gone bankrupt trying to make films in Nanking. The new Motion Picture Department of the Commercial Press immediately set about making several costume films, including one or two presenting the actor Mei Lan-fang in excerpts from some of his plays. They were shot in a banker's house in Peking, but never publicly shown. In 1918 the Universal Film Company of America sent a team on location to China, and at the end of their trip the equipment was sold to the Commercial Press, whose studio facilities were greatly improved as a result.

Around 1920 several small studios were founded in Shanghai, including the Shanghai Motion Picture Company, directed by Tan Tu-yu. His wife Yin Ming-chu played the lead in *The Great Oath* made in 1921, one of the first full-length Chinese films. The New Asia Motion Picture Company founded by the Yin brothers was another early studio, and the Star Motion Picture Company founded in 1922 became one of the largest in China. The success of Star's first production, *An Orphan Saves His Grandfather*, resulted in several wealthy Shanghai businessmen investing in films, although the company nearly went bankrupt making the picture, and Chou Chien-yun, the vice-president, was rumoured to have borrowed his wife's dowry to subsidise the production. The orphan fortunately saved much more than his grandfather and gave the film industry a morale boost.

The period between 1922 and 1926 was one of rapid growth and competition. At the height of the boom there were nearly a hundred companies operating in the Shanghai area, although many of them were here today and gone tomorrow. They did little to improve the standard of Chinese films, which were treated simply as a commodity for speculation. By the mid-thirties most of these concerns had disappeared, and there were only half a dozen companies left.

One of these was the T'ien I Motion Picture Company

which made early experiments with synchronisation and in 1931 produced its first sound film, *Clear Sky after Rain*. In the same year the Star Motion Picture Company also produced its first "talkie," *Singing Peony*, featuring Hu Tieh, or Miss Butterfly (see Plate 5). The story was about Red Peony, an actress blessed with both beauty and a fine singing voice. Her mother prevented her marrying her lover, a fur dealer, and insisted on a union with the brother of the theatre owner who employed Red Peony. The new bridegroom immediately began sponging on his wife and eventually stole her jewellery to give to his cabaret-girl paramour. Red Peony was so distressed when she found out that she became sick, lost her voice, and, in consequence, her employment. On the advice of an evil friend, her husband then sold their daughter to a sing-song house, but was smitten with remorse and helped his wife get the child back. He killed his evil counsellor, and was imprisoned for the crime. The three-hour film ended with a shot of Red Peony, escorted by her faithful lover, the fur dealer, sadly embarking to take a job in Dairen.

A Chinese critic wrote of the film, "The sound registry is not clear, pronunciation of the national mandarin accent is artificial and mixed with dialect . . . scenes are inartistic and inaccurate, for instance, a clock always points to three, lighting is too strong, the sixth and seventh reels could have been omitted. There is a lack of climax." Severe censure indeed, but it probably did not worry the ordinary filmgoers who loved pictures of this kind and the longer the better.

Hu Tieh and Hung Shen, the actress and scriptwriter involved in this film, both have a niche in early film history. Hu Tieh was of Cantonese parentage but received her education in Peking and Shanghai. At the age of seventeen, she was accepted by the Chung Hua Film Company for a course of training, and quickly attracted attention by her looks and ability. The Star Motion Picture

Company signed her up in 1925, and she became their principal actress, making more than twenty films for them. One of her most popular pictures, *Two Sisters*, directed by Cheng Cheng-ch'iu, earned her the title of Movie Queen in 1934. The next year as the *doyenne* of Chinese film actresses she was invited to an international film congress in Moscow and travelled there with Mei Lan-fang, who had also been invited to Russia with his troupe. In April 1936 she travelled on to Europe in Mei's company and visited Italy, France, and England where she toured the film studios. She returned to Shanghai to be married and left for Hong Kong with her husband when war broke out in 1937. When the Japanese occupied the British colony she escaped to Chungking, returning to Shanghai after the war and to Hong Kong when the Communists came to power.

After her husband's death in 1958, she returned to the studios and by 1961 had played four leading roles in films produced by the Shaw Brothers studio in Hong Kong. Miss Butterfly has emerged from her chrysalis a second time, and although she now plays matronly roles befitting her age, she remains the only one of the stars left from those far-off days who continues to satisfy her public.

Hung Shen was actor, director, playwright, and critic in the course of his professional career. He came from Kiangsu and after graduating in Peking studied at both Ohio and Harvard Universities. On returning to Shanghai in 1922 he taught literature, but was elected a member of the Shanghai Dramatic Club in 1923 and given leading roles in plays by Ou-yang Yü-ch'ien and Hu Shih. From then on he gave his life to the theatre. As the Dramatic Club's director he was the first to use a mixed cast, a novel step in those days. When a Harold Lloyd comedy showing the Chinese as a race of gangsters was screened at an International Settlement cinema in 1930, Hung Shen stood up and publicly denounced the film as a reflection on his people. It required some spirit for a Chinese to do such a thing in those surroundings, and Hung Shen was arrested for it.

After 1930 he devoted much time to film work and in 1932 the Star company sent him to Hollywood to study technical methods. On his return to China he produced a film called *Peach Blossoms after the Storm* which made a great impression with its anti-Japanese theme. Hung Shen is remembered as a director-scriptwriter who made his mark at a time when Chinese films were steadily acquiring a more national flavour.

One of the best known early film actors was Wang Yüan-lung (1903–60). He started his career as a student in a military academy but deserted the uniform for a life in films. He co-starred with Hu Tieh, in whose first picture he appeared. He specialised in character roles in his later years and was a great favourite with filmgoers. He left Shanghai in 1949 but continued his profession in Hong Kong and was active in the studios there until shortly before his death.

Another famous Star company actress was Yang Nai-mei, whose classic features were once the toast of Chinese filmgoers from Shanghai to Tientsin. She eventually ran her own company, the Yang Nai Corporation, and starred in its first film, *The Wonderful Girl*, in 1928.

A list of stars like these could run on for several paragraphs. There were dozens who commanded an ardent following, lived their lives in public, and were in general the focus of the same kind of romantic nonsense that surrounded their Hollywood contemporaries. Nevertheless, the Chinese film actress did a lot to help break down the prejudices against women performers, and this was an achievement.

Considering all the circumstances, some reasonably competent pictures were turned out in the old days, although the general average was not so high as it might have been, and artistic development was hindered by the producers' anxiety to get quick returns. Studios were small, makeshift, and often poorly equipped. Cameras, machinery, and negatives were all American imports. Producers and directors tended to economise at the expense of the picture, and technical defects were often ignored in order to avoid re-takes. The greatest Western criticism was the Chinese reluctance to cut adequately. Shanghai film makers on an average cut their negatives by half, where Western films were often cut to less than a quarter of the original length. The ordinary Chinese film ran to about 10,000 feet and was often marked by the use of unsuitable dramatic conventions, an addiction to lachrymose sentimentality, and a passion for long-windedness at the expense of action.

The most popular pictures were usually those with a contemporary theme, preferably tragic when it concerned women's position in society. Typical was *Woman* made by the Yi Hua Motion Picture Company in 1934 and acclaimed the picture of the year. The story concerned Yi, Ling, and Yu, three student friends. Yi was expelled from college when the principal discovered she had been a dance hostess. Ling's protests at her friend's treatment were so icily received that she went off to study medicine at another college. Yu, on the other hand, married, but her husband became infatuated with a cabaret girl on whom he lavished his money and time until he finally lost his job. He had to pawn his child's birthday gifts to get money; his wife dismissed their servant; and, final blow, her father who lived with them in the approved Chinese custom was forced to take work as a hotel porter. To get money to pay for her sick child's medical care Yu appealed to her former college mate Yi, by now the concubine of a wealthy man. Yi found a post for her friend with a real estate firm whose manager tried to compromise his new employee in a hotel. His improper advances were averted by the arrival of a porter who turned out to be Yu's father. Disaster followed fast, for she arrived home to find her house had burned down and her child had perished in the flames. And when her father returned to taunt her with her "loose" conduct, she could bear no more and committed suicide.

In the late thirties a new attitude developed towards film making. By then dramatists like T'ien Han, Ou-yang Yü-ch'ien, and Hung Shen had all worked for the cinema and brought a greater artistry and, incidentally, a greater political awareness to the scripts. In addition there was a drive to recruit talented stage artists for the screen. One of the most brilliant actresses of the period was Pai Yang (see Plate 6), who was so much in demand that she was invited to work for two different studios and offered three leading parts as soon as she gave up her stage career. Her first film, *At the Crossroads*, made in 1937, used the unemployment problem as a theme and was one of several pictures that showed recognition of social issues. But most of all in this period the film became an important propaganda weapon against the Japanese after their seizure of Manchuria and their continued hostility towards China.

In the Shanghai studios there was a tacit understanding that "national defence themes" would be stressed. Censorship complications prevented anything other than indirect reference and symbolism in films, but there was no doubt in Chinese eyes as to whom and what was intended. The villain of the picture might be human or animal, but he was always shown attacking homes or territory only to receive his just deserts at the hands of the sufferers. One such picture was *Brave Hunters* which represented Chinese villagers menaced by a wolf pack which attacked their homes. At first they went to a quack for advice on how to deal with the peril, but finally they followed the advice of the village hero who by a well-organised plan of attack effectively dealt with the wolves. According to one Chinese critic this film worried the Shanghai Municipal Council censors, who were chary of offending the Japanese. They called in the Japanese censor. But he passed the film, refusing to believe that wolves could symbolise his people.

The outbreak of war in 1937 disrupted the organisation of the film industry. The "big four" motion picture companies in Shanghai at the time were the Star, the United Photoplay, the Hsin Hua, and the Yi Hua. In Nanking there was the Central Motion Picture Studio, a government propaganda-educational agency founded in July 1935. When the Nationalist Government evacuated to Chungking the studio went with them and became a unit of the China Motion Picture Corporation. This subsidiary of the Political Department of the National Military Council was originally intended as a propaganda unit in the campaign to suppress the Communists. After the outbreak of war it was re-organised as the main film production and distribution body in non-occupied China.

When the war came a number of Shanghai screen actors left to join travelling dramatic troupes in the interior, but hundreds of others made patriotic films under government sponsorship in Chungking. Although they had been the hardened participants in many a screen struggle with corrupt officials, grasping landlords, and all the other evil personalities of the old days, this was the first time they had been able to show their contempt for the Japanese openly, and they set about it with gusto. Some of these early war films would have puzzled European audiences as to which side they were on, for the Chinese army of those days wore steel helmets of German origin.

A famous combat film was *Fight to the Last*, about a Chinese brigade commander with a brilliant military record. He fought bravely in the trenches, although he knew his wife and father had been killed and his home destroyed. Even when he was seriously wounded he refused to give up and urged his men to forget personal considerations. The climax came when his battered forces rushed the enemy lines and won the battle in bitter hand-to-hand combat. A second popular war film was *The Doomed*

Battalion, inspired by an episode in the Japanese attack on Shanghai. The picture opened with a girl entertainer singing the "Song of the Doomed Battalion" in a teahouse. Amid the vociferous applause of the guests the camera then faded in to bitter fighting around a large Chapei warehouse, and refugees stampeding before Japanese bayonets. In the warehouse, a beleaguered garrison of five hundred men sniped at the Japanese and drove back two enemy platoons with hand grenades. Yang Huimin, a heroic girl guide, tried to carry a Nationalist flag across the Soochow Creek in a sampan. Her frail craft was capsized by a bomb, but, nothing daunted, she swam on to the opposite shore and finally reached the marooned warehouse where, amid defiant cheers, the last Chinese flag was hoisted over Shanghai.

Elementary in their emotional appeal and using all the old melodramatic tricks, these films could scarcely be regarded as great cinema art, though they were no worse than the war pictures of other countries on that score. They met a mood of the times, and thousands of Chinese applauded their sentiments.

Until war broke out between Japan and the West in 1941, a good deal of Chinese film production continued in Shanghai even though the government studios had moved to Chungking. Between 1939–41 producers in general had concentrated more on historical films with a nationalistic appeal or modern themes in a lighter vein, rather than on war subjects. Chinese producers had always depended a great deal on the Southeast Asian market where colonial governments were still wary of offending the Japanese, and so it was necessary to play down war sentiments. A popular film of this era was *Mu Lan Joins the Army,* starring Ch'en Yun-shang, a screen favourite of girl students in those days. The story was about a Chinese warrior maiden, famous in historical legend and incidentally a popular character on the Peking stage. A second costume film of the day was *Empress Wu,* a "super production" based on a story about the famous T'ang Empress who single-handedly ruled China. She was played by Violet Koo (Ku Lan-chün), another star of the period who has long ago entered the limbo of forgotten screen idols.

A more contemporary picture was *Glorious on Parade,* made by the Tati Motion Picture Corporation, a company founded in Hong Kong in 1939 by T. Y. Lo of the government-controlled China Motion Picture Corporation to meet the demand for films with less intense war stories. *Glorious on Parade* was about two labourer friends in Hong Kong who refused to load a ship destined for an enemy port. A fight ensued with the foreman, and one of them was sent to jail. On his release he discovered his friend working as a sandwich-board man. One night the two men rescued a servant girl who was being beaten by her mistress and gave her shelter in their home. To help with her upkeep and unknown to her benefactors, she became a strip-tease dancer, but they discovered her secret and persuaded her to resign. The cabaret manager proved difficult, but under threats from the two men was forced to comply with their demands. Then, realising the uselessness of their lives in the city, the two men and the girl set off for free China to work for their country's good.

The last uneasy days before Pearl Harbor also saw the Shanghai production of China's first full-length cartoon film, *Princess Iron Fan,* based on the famous classical novel *Journey to the West* and featuring pig and monkey characters popular in Chinese mythology (see Plate 7). The cartoon was strongly influenced by Walt Disney, but it had its own Chinese flavour which suggested promising developments had not the extension of the war in 1941 put an end to such projects.

After its wartime dispersal the Chinese film industry returned to Shanghai in 1945, and production slowly started up again. Many films of the immediate post-war period remained coloured by the sentimental-patriotic spirit of the preceding years. The writer recalls sitting through a saga about the war years which was screened in Shanghai in 1947 and entailed going out for dinner after the matinee and returning to see the second half of the film in the evening. Cutting and editing were still conditioned by an oriental conception of time.

The tragi-comic romances in which the Shanghai school specialised were soon in full swing again, but besides these frothy productions there were one or two productions that indicated some progress in post-war film making. *The Spring River Flows East*, starring Pai Yang, a sensitively treated domestic tragedy with a typical Chinese wife-mistress situation, indicated a new grasp of film potentialities. Again this was a long picture which ran in two parts. There were others which showed new advances in the use of film and promise for the future, but cinema production became too unequal a struggle in the rapidly deteriorating political situation.

In 1948 the first colour film was made: the actor Mei Lan-fang in his play *Sheng Szu Hen*, anglicised as *Wedding in a Dream*. The colour photography was poor, and the general lack of electric current in Nanking and Shanghai in 1948–49 made every showing a hazard. Technically unsuccessful, *Wedding in a Dream* could almost be regarded as the swan song of the old film industry in China before the downfall of the Nationalist Government.

After 1949, Hong Kong, whose film industry before the war was on a much smaller scale than Shanghai's, began to develop as a new and active centre augmented by many directors, producers, and stars who settled there after the Communists took Shanghai. Today, Hong Kong has a large film colony, a number of busy studios, and turns out a quantity of pictures each year in both the Cantonese and Kuoyü dialects. They are aimed primarily at the Southeast Asian market, and the biggest investors in the Hong Kong film industry are the Shaw brothers from Singapore who not very long ago built a $5,000,000 studio in Hong Kong to replace their old concern. The tycoons of the Southeast Asian film world, the Shaw brothers have carried out an ambitious programme of film production, both colour and black-and-white, within recent years. But while Hong Kong films achieve a high standard of technical proficiency and have carried off several awards at Asian film festivals, they have made no really outstanding contribution to Chinese film art. *Back Door*, a Shaw production judged the best picture of the seventh Asian Film Festival, in which Hu Tieh made her film comeback supported by a talented cast, was merely a nostalgic re-creation of the old Shanghai spirit. Its portrayal of human values was hackneyed, and it lacked contemporary significance. The Hong Kong film industry is dedicated to light entertainment; as a serious artistic force it has very little to say.

THE CONTEMPORARY SCENE IN CHINA

In 1949 the Communists energetically set about re-organising the dormant film world in China. A Bureau of Cinematographic Art was established at the Ministry of Cultural Affairs, with supervision of all film studios in northeastern China, Peking, and Shanghai. Prior to 1949 the Communists had taken over the old Changchun Film Company, founded in Manchukuo days and run by the Japanese during the war. This studio produced nine documentaries between 1947–48. In January 1949, the Communists took over the Nationalists' Central Motion Picture Studio in Peking, and in May five Shanghai studios were made public property and amalgamated as the New Shanghai Film Production Company. A five-year programme was laid down in 1950: 26 feature films, one technicolour feature, 48 newsreels, 40 reprints of dubbed Soviet films, and 36 reprints of Soviet educational films. Ten years later the official production figures were given as 103 feature films, 10 cartoon films, 151 dubbed foreign films, 18 full-length documentaries, and 552 shorts, which gives some indication of the growth and expansion of film work in China.

The major centres are now in Peking and Shanghai, each city having four feature film studios. In Shanghai there is a cartoon film studio and one for dubbing; Peking has a newsreel studio; and there are scientific-educational film studios in both cities. Sian, Canton, and Changchun each has a feature film studio, and in 1960 a cinema academy was established in Changchun and a Cinema Art Research Institute in Peking. Touring projection units are used for taking films to rural areas, and in 1960 their official total was given as 18,500. Personnel employed in film work were given as 90,000 in 1960 as against 3,000 in 1950, a measure of how seriously the Communists are taking film production and a rough estimate of present-day resources. What then of the production itself?

Naturally all the possibilities of the film medium have been devoted to propaganda for the Communist regime and its achievements. Themes dealing with the revolution, progress in industry, agricultural production, and so on, have proliferated from the national studios. The first full-length feature film produced by the Changchun studios in 1949, for example, was *The Bridge*, the story of a group of workers who helped Communist troops rebuild in record time a bridge destroyed by the Nationalists. In 1950 the Peking Film Studio produced a forty-five-minute documentary entitled *The Birth of the New China*, which traced the events leading to the inauguration of the Communist Government and opened with shots of Mao Tse-tung addressing the Chinese Peoples' Political Consultative Council on September 21, 1949. As a Communist columnist put it: "His voice is powerful, and the sound recording excellent." The same writer's statement that the film "occupies a unique position in the history of Chinese filmdom and will remain one of the few treasures of the world," may not command unanimous agreement, but certainly the picture will be a historic piece of documentation like several others of this period.

Other typical films of the early fifties were *Woman Locomotive Driver*, based on the life story of Tien Kuei-ying, China's first woman engine driver; *Sing Aloud and Advance*, a story of Chao Kuo-yu, the worker who later became Director of the All China Federation of Labour's Production Department; *Brightness*, which concerned power-plant rehabilitation; and *Unite, Fight for a New Day*, which was about a textile mill strike under the Nationalists.

The list could go on. The quality of some of these early films is best summed up in the words of a Communist journalist: "Not all these films reach the high level of the best. It could hardly be expected with up to 80 per cent of the artists newcomers in film making. The most fundamental shortcomings, however, stem from the fact that producers have too often conceived their material and action in terms of the theatrical stage rather than the cinema with its tremendous resources of depth in time and space. . . ." It was a familiar cry and revealed the problem that has beset Chinese films from the beginning. There has been constant conflict in trying to fuse the realism of the camera with the non-realistic acting conventions of the traditional stage in such a way that something more than the gross sentimentality, stereotyped characterisation, and unsuitable melodrama from which so many Chinese films have suffered in the past will be achieved.

A happy example of the process in reverse, the adaptation of traditional acting techniques to cinema, was seen in the film *Liang Shan-po and Chu Ying-t'ai* made at the Shanghai studios and directed by Sang Hu and Huang Sha, which was shown in London in 1955. The first colour film to reach the West from Communist China, it was based on a traditional Shaohsing drama and played by an all-female cast, a custom of this particular style of theatre.

The film was successful from every point of view. The

theatrical framework was preserved, and the spoken dialogue, solo songs, and connecting choral passages sung off screen were convincingly blended. The cast sustained the conventions of the play without making it incongruous as film action. The decor was deliberately conventional and subdued in the manner of Chinese painting, with only a few exterior shots. Direction was straightforward, with some lengthy individual takes, and nothing was allowed to intervene between the performers. In spite of its length and unusual idiom, the film achieved a poetic intensity on the screen and a freshness of style that marked it as an outstanding production. It was marred by a climax in which two butterflies flitted over a grave and the shot relapsed into the tawdry realism of the painted stage set, an example of the curious insensitivity to incongruity that seems to afflict the Chinese on occasion. It is possibly a legacy from their old theatre where the dividing line between the sublime and the ridiculous is frequently very slender and defined only by the subtlety of artistic conventions.

Films of traditional plays with leading stage actors are now a regular feature of Chinese film production, and many of them are exceedingly well done. A general criticism would be that they use too realistic sets. On the whole, films like these make an esoteric appeal to Western audiences, and there has been nothing yet in this genre to surpass the 1955 production described above. In 1959 the Shanghai studios tried to take matters a step further with their production of *The Magic Lotus Lantern*, a dance drama based on an old legend. The action throughout was performed entirely in dance and mime with no dialogue and combined the technique of Western ballet, especially in the group scenes, with traditional Chinese choreography. The experiment was by no means successful and on occasion flawed by the rather crude realism of the sets noted elsewhere. Even so the film had its moments, and the Chinese regard it as an experiment.

It is natural that many new Chinese films with contemporary themes show obvious respect for Soviet models. But from a technical standpoint recently made films are far more sophisticated in every way than Chinese films have ever been before, even if their dramatic content tends to be naive by our standards. Photography, colour, continuity, and editing are in general greatly advanced in present-day Chinese films, and, although they are far from matching the experienced techniques of the world's greatest film makers, a new stage of development is apparent in the Chinese cinema. China has not yet produced her Kurosawa, Bergmann, or even her Eisenstein, but directors are emerging with a new sense of their medium.

One of the major productions of 1959 was the film *Storm*, directed by Ching San who adapted the script from his own stage play and also acted the principal role. He is one of the more promising of the new studio personalities. The story of the film is based on the Peking-Hankow railway strike of 1922–23, and Ching San has attempted to give a traditional theatrical accent to an essentially cinematic treatment of his subject. Although the restraints of propaganda tend to make some sequences contrived, the picture achieves an artistic unity and a more stimulating fusion of acting patterns than has been seen before.

Another major production in 1960 was the colour film *Lin Tse-hsii*, the story of the Opium War. Bound by its very subject to be a violently nationalistic film, it was not aggressively anti-British in purpose and conveyed its story with a convincing sense of the issues to be analysed. Directed by Cheng Chun-i and Tseng Fan, with the veteran actor Chao Tan in the title role, it was an ambitious contemporary approach to a historical theme.

Communist China's first wide-screen production, *New Story of an Old Soldier*, directed by Shen Fu, with the pre-war actor Tsui Wei in the principal role, also appeared in 1960. The story concerned an army veteran's struggle to reclaim agricultural land in northeast China, and Tsui Wei as a rough and ready but extremely lovable character was convincingly sympathetic. The propaganda message of the film, "that the hero achieved his aim because he mobilised and relied on the masses of the people under the leadership of the party," was overshadowed by Tsui Wei's individual interpretation. Western European critics who saw this film were favourably impressed in spite of the propaganda. (All the pictures named above have been shown in London.)

Within the last few years emphasis has been laid on making cartoon films for children. In the Shanghai studios some of the recent leading spirits have been the Wan brothers, Lai-ming, Ku-chan, and Chao-chen, who made *Princess Iron Fan* in 1940, and joined the Shanghai studios from Hong Kong in 1954. In 1958 they produced a new style of cartoon made with animated cutouts based on traditional shadow theatre and paper cutting. The first production in this technique was *The Pig and the Watermelon* based on an incident from the classical novel *Journey to the West*, which also inspired the Wan brothers' first cartoon film.

Although the new cartoon films are devised to convey a "good" moral, in a majority of cases this is no more obvious than in the contents of children's tales anywhere, and it would be difficult to particularise them as political propaganda. Traditional legends and folk stories inspire many of them, but contemporary subjects are not ignored. They range through a variety of techniques, from downright imitation of Disney to versions of Russian and Czechoslovakian puppet films. A recent development was the cartoon film *Hsiao K'o Tou Chao Ma Ma* (Little Frog in Search of Mama), made in 1960 and based upon the painting style of the old traditional artist Ch'i Pai-shih. A second film inspired by the horse paintings of the modern artist Hsü Pei-hung is scheduled; there are possibilities here which argue well for an original and refined cartoon treatment.

The film is a dynamic medium, a tool by which the artist is able to enter the relatively unexplored world of visual movement. It is the art of the twentieth century, a new art largely unhampered by the restraints of tradition and therefore one that holds special promise for the changing societies of the Orient. It is possible to argue that as an art of communication the film is unrivalled as propaganda and that this is the main purpose it serves in a controlled society. But Russia, for example, has to her credit some of the century's greatest film achievements.

A new Soviet film was recently criticised in the *New York Times* by Brooks Atkinson as follows: "Socialist realism, which is the official art dogma that Stalin laid down in 1934, is responsible for the dismal fact that Russian literature has ceased to have world significance. It has become too parochial for other parts of the world; it is also sterile in the opinion of some Russians. Yet here is a little masterpiece of film art that seems not to be imprisoned within the framework of dogma . . . a realistic film based on the simple dignity of the Russian people, and it is as spontaneous as anything produced in the West. Socialist realism is only a cant phrase when talented professionals find a theme that is universally acceptable. . . ."

There are parallels in this that can well be applied to China. Though still behind in film achievement, the possibility exists that in this medium she will attain her greatest artistic regeneration.

V. PAINTING AND THE GRAPHIC ARTS

Painting and calligraphy represent the highest forms of artistic accomplishment in China, and the two are interrelated. The spontaneous technique of the painter is dependent on the same kind of manual dexterity that is needed to master the writing of hundreds of characters. Successful "ink-play" is a vital principle of Chinese painting; the brush must be controlled with an effortless strength that allows an instantaneous expression of mood. Harmony is the most important word in the vocabulary of Chinese art, and the painter must be in spiritual harmony with his subject. In the past this meant inspiration through the quieter rhythms of nature rather than through the dynamic activity of the human world. And of all kinds of painting landscape was regarded as supreme. In landscape the painter identified himself the most completely with nature and indulged his technical perfection in a meditative unity that was the ideal of Chinese pictorial design.

Although painting and calligraphy are twin arts and often complementary, a picture being combined with a written poem, calligraphy has always been valued by the Chinese as a great art in its own right. Brush-written characters are enjoyed independently for their abstract beauty and subtle conjunction of structure, line, and rhythm. Examples of calligraphy are hung on Chinese walls in the same way as paintings. Fine calligraphy is an art that requires time to learn, years to become skilful in, and a lifetime to become a master of. These are not facts easily reconciled with the ordinary pattern of living in the twentieth century, and the practice of calligraphy has waned

85

in consequence. The inventions of the fountain pen and typewriter have done a great deal to accelerate the decline.

None of the busy young Chinese professors who throng American universities today would think of using a brush in their academic work, and even if it were practical few of them *could* do so with any degree of skill. The necessity for a modern bi-lingual education has helped many younger Chinese to forget the old traditions. This is particularly noticeable in a place like Hong Kong where school children must acquire a command of English equal to that of their own tongue. They have no time for the intensive study of calligraphy. And at home the modern Hong Kong schoolboy as like as not spends his leisure hours watching Westerns on the television. He has not the same incentive for the daily hours of practice his elders were expected to undergo in their homes. Against this let it be said that there have always been bad handwriters in China as in every country. Supremacy in a tradition need not blind us to the fact that the Chinese are human like anyone else! Nevertheless the extraordinary importance of calligraphy in Chinese culture cannot be emphasised too much, especially in its relationship to painting.

But the calligraphic nature of his painting holds certain pitfalls for the Chinese artist. The technique leads him to rely implicitly on well-tried forms at the moment of creation and does not encourage experiment. This, and the fact that all Chinese artists learn their craft by faithfully copying the masters, is apt to narrow the painter's scope. Instead of constantly seeking inspiration from the masters' sources, he is tempted to imitate their manner alone. At worst this becomes empty repetition and the artist simply a copyist, albeit a technically skilled one. It is no coincidence that Chinese painting has produced some of the most accomplished fakes in art history. He would be a rash man indeed who believed everything Chinese dealers told him!

A walk round any ordinary traditional painting exhibition of the kind that may still be seen in Hong Kong,

Taiwan, or Singapore today, and was common in China before 1949, would reveal an endless repetition of mountain landscapes, bamboos, or blossoms, which perpetuate mannerisms of the brush and show the vacuum into which painting falls if it is dependent for too long upon bravura. Indifferent painting in every country is dull; the technical level of conformity makes it peculiarly so in China. It was revolt against such sterility that drove a younger school of artists to experiment with Western methods after 1911.

The history of painting in China since then has been one of divided loyalties and open rivalry between traditional technique and Western method, meaning oil painting. Soon after the May Fourth Movement, a few young Chinese artists went abroad to study. Like art students everywhere, Paris was their goal, and once there it was perhaps inevitable that oil painting hypnotised their imaginations. Many of them in their anxiety to become completely Western learnt oil painting on the principle that it was first important to acquire a style. So they copied first one Western painter and then another, never stopping to consider whether a re-appraisal of their own mediums could have served them better in seeking a new vision. Nor did they realise that in their own calligraphic tradition and respect for abstract form they in fact possessed qualities that placed them on a par with some of the new ideas then stirring Western art. They imitated, for all the wrong reasons, academicians, impressionists, postimpressionists, and cubists, encompassing the gamut of European painting. But out of it all came little that was Chinese.

The returned Chinese student of Western painting had other problems, a major one being his lack of communication with the West. Distances were great, travel was expensive, and the great era of official cultural relations was yet to come. The foreign community in pre-war China scarcely offered an effective background of contemporary artistic interest. At no time was there ever a major exhibition of Western painting in Shanghai, nothing comparable to the 1934 Chinese exhibition in London for example. Chinese artists were starved of contacts. Even the few men who had been to Europe remained cut off from the main stream of Western development once they had returned, and with few exceptions they could only sigh nostalgically for the days of artistic adventure behind them.

Artists in China today are starved of contacts in another sense; directed in their contacts would possibly be a more appropriate term, and this is discussed later in the chapter. Outside their homeland there are one or two Chinese artists today who have found a place in contemporary Western art without abandoning their own past. It may well be that someday these men and women will be channels through which a new creative phase in painting will develop in China.

During the thirty years or so that Chinese painters experimented freely with Western techniques, that is to say in the period before 1949, there always remained a majority faithful to the traditional style. This included those who allowed Western ideas to influence their essentially Chinese methods and those who refused to make any compromise with the West at all. Among the men who abandoned themselves completely to Western technique there were one or two who attained great competence, but it is significant that none of them ever completely renounced the national style and several later in their careers reverted to it completely.

Among the traditional-style painters there were a number of distinguished men at work who brought a fresh eye and new vigour to old methods. It is not possible to list them all here, but in the careers of the four traditional painters described in the following paragraphs a general idea of the main trends may be gathered, for each man was representative in his own way.

Until the Sino-Japanese War, Peking was the centre of traditional-style painting; Shanghai, Nanking, and Canton were the cities where the modern experimental movements were the most active. This was a pattern that also applied to other arts, although Peking was a lively focus for new literary developments—the May Fourth Movement, after all, began there. But Peking remained the old cultural capital and a stronghold of the accepted forms of painting and theatre in particular. The traditional painters of pre-war Peking were more concerned with the respective merits of the Northern academic style and the Southern free style than with any more startling innovations. These classifications in fact had no geographical meaning but were used rather in the sense of "right" and "left," if such distinctions can be applied to styles that were centuries old and primarily concerned with long established forms and not political differences.

The *doyen* of the Northern style was Prince P'u Ju (1887–) who was a cousin of P'u Yi, the last of the Emperors of China. He was brought up from childhood among the famous Palace collection of old paintings of which he had an extensive knowledge. He embodied a Chinese theory that the true man of culture comes from a wealthy background because only there can he get understanding of the best art which automatically accompanies status. Conservative to a degree, P'u Ju followed a tradition handed down through generations of Court painters. His pure colour, exquisite precision of ink tones, and delicate brushwork were modelled on the finest of the old masters and represented a distilled art completely remote from the outside world. P'u Ju had two brothers, P'u Ch'üan and P'u Chin, both equally adept painters in the Court tradition. It is worth noting that one of the most interesting contemporary Chinese artists in a contemporary idiom, Tseng Yu-ho of Honolulu, was a pupil of P'u Chin.

In direct contrast to Prince P'u Ju was Ch'i Pai-shih (1863–1957), the leader of the Southern school and a remarkable old man now accounted one of the great masters of the century. He started life as the carpenter of a peasant family in Hunan. From carpentry he turned to wood-carving and then to painting. There is no time within living memory when Ch'i Pai-shih did not seem a patriarch of painting, for he was an old man before the Japanese war but lived on to become one of the most honoured painters in Communist China. Until he was in his fifties he had only a local reputation, but after that his work became nationally prized and finally, in his last years, internationally known. His style is remarkable for its bold and forceful vision and a tremendous vitality of brushwork. After a lifetime of single-minded application he attained a new force within the traditions of his art. In the later part of his career he liked to paint crabs, shrimps, insects, gourds, and the blossoms known in English as "morning glory," of which he was an expert cultivator. The loving sympathy, humour, and gaiety underlying these paintings mark them as the creations of a man with an intensely personal vision.

Because of his background and achievements the Communists inevitably made a great fuss over Ch'i, and he was elevated to the status of a national "cultural treasure." But long before 1949 Ch'i had become a highly successful painter who did not lack patrons. After the war he had a great vogue among the foreign community in China, to whom, it was reported, he always sold paintings by the square foot.

At the age of fifty-seven he took a concubine who later succeeded his wife on her death. Old Ch'i was thrifty and industrious in his manner of living, according to Chinese moral precepts. In his long gown, black skull cap, and with his wispy white beard, he was a revered figure among his own people. Ch'i was also a poet, seal engraver, and calligrapher of distinction; indeed he always claimed that his painting was inferior to his other accomplishments. But this may be regarded as the permissible false modesty of a great artist.

Another type of traditional painter is Chang Ta-ch'ien (1899–   ), from Szechwan. He was first taught his craft by his mother, herself a painter. In his late teens he studied painting on textiles in Kyoto, Japan. In 1919 Chang spent a period in a Buddhist monastery whose abbot was a poet-calligrapher-painter. After leaving this retreat Chang spent a year in Shanghai studying under the noted painter Li Jui-ching, who also taught him calligraphy. Li died, and Chang returned to Szechwan where he remained until 1926, studying the works of two monk painters, Shih T'ao (Tao Ch'i, 1630–c.1707) and Pa-ta Shan-jen (Chu Ta, 1626–c.1705), both of whom had a lasting influence on his work. In 1927 he began to travel extensively throughout China, visiting the mountains, lakes, and gorges made famous by the old masters, which he began to record in his own paintings. In 1931 he and his brother were sent as official delegates to an exhibition of classical Japanese paintings held in Japan. In the following year he settled in the old city of Soochow for a period and kept a pet tiger and monkeys. But he was soon off again, this time to Peking, for Chang is possessed with the restlessness typical of many artists of his kind. He was in Peking when the Japanese came, and they detained him on parole, but he managed to escape to Chungking.

During the war he made an intensive study of the Buddhist Tunhuang Caves in northwest China. His copies of the cave paintings, numbering more than two hundred, were first exhibited in 1944 and caused a considerable sensation in the art world. It was the first time that these old Buddhist masterpieces had been recorded for the public. The period spent in Tunhuang had considerable influence on Chang's own painting, and he did a whole series of figure studies whose style shows his debt to the Buddhist frescoes.

In 1948, Chang left China before the Communists came to power. In 1950, he was invited to India and held exhibitions there, and in 1952 he made his home in South America. In 1956, he started his travels once again, making his first trip to Europe where he had an exhibition in the Musée d'Art Moderne in Paris. While he was in France, he was the guest of Picasso at his villa La Californie.

Chang now lives in Brazil but emerges regularly to travel abroad; it is impossible for him to remain static for too long. His most recent trip was his second visit to Paris in 1961 when he had an exhibition and was interviewed by André Masson for L'Express. His work is highly regarded in France, where one of his lotus paintings was bought by the Musée du Jeu de Paume, Paris, as early as 1933.

Chang Ta-ch'ien is a bearded, flamboyant character with a great reputation as a gourmet. As an artist he represents what might be called the "eclectic" school of Chinese painting. He is a tremendous virtuoso, able to paint in several different classical styles with equal skill and aplomb. The story is told that he once purchased an old master that was in fact a copy made by himself, but which he failed to detect on a second acquaintance. It is apocryphal, no doubt, but typical of the reputation he has acquired. Chinese connoisseurs nevertheless have a profound respect for Chang's work because of the sincere homage he pays to their national heritage. He is popular with some admirers for his paintings of women that show the strong influence of his Tunhuang phase, but his most representative works are landscapes and large, bold renderings of lotus and other flowers.

In 1916, Canton, the home of the Chinese revolution, became the centre of a painting movement which retained all the technical methods of the traditional style but incorporated certain Western ideas and principles. The leaders of this "revolutionary" painting were Kao Chien-fu (1879–1951) and his brother Kao Ch'i-feng (1889–1933) who had both studied in Japan and worked for Sun Yat-sen in the early days of the revolution. As a matter of fact Chien-fu was offered political advancement when the Republic was formed, but declined it in favour of a life devoted to fostering a new national style of painting.

Briefly, Kao Chien-fu's theories were that a new style of Chinese painting could be created by retaining the vitality of the Chinese brush-and-ink technique but supplementing it with the Western use of perspective and light and shade. In order to create "revolutionary" painting, he considered it necessary to rely not only on the form and technique of the painting but also on its motive, that is, its subject matter. In the modern age this meant incorporating all the trappings of industrialised civilisation as subjects for painting—railways, telegraph poles, and even aeroplanes. Kao was the first artist to use an aeroplane as a motif in a traditional scroll-type painting (see Plate 8). It was called *Flying in the Rain,* and the Chinese critic Wen Yuan-ning wrote of it in 1936: "Mr. Kao is a revolutionary in politics. In an artist so truly one with himself as Mr. Kao is, it would be strange if we did not find a revolutionary in art also. But such he is. His daring in drawing a motor car crossing a bridge in one picture of his, and an aeroplane in *Flying in the Rain,* gives obvious evidence of this quality in him. To paint a motor car or an aeroplane may not qualify an artist to be styled a revolutionary in Western art, but it certainly does so in Chinese art. A revolutionary artist must, however, be distinguished from a cranky one. A revolutionary develops his art, while a cranky artist bungles his. A Chinese artist drawing an aeroplane or a motor car in the Chinese manner runs great risks of being a crank. That we do not feel anything cranky in *Flying in the Rain* shows Mr. Kao's success in incorporating new motives into his work."

Kao started a school of art, the Ch'un Shui School, which became a flourishing centre in 1916. He gathered round him a group of followers who were later known as the Lingnan School, because Kao was teaching at Lingnan University, Canton, in the heyday of the movement. During the early years of the Sino-Japanese War the Lingnan painters made a considerable stir with their pictures depicting bomb damage, homeless refugees, and other themes of military destruction.

Kao Chien-fu was an active propagandist in the cause of new painting, and in 1929 organised the first National Exhibition of Chinese Art held at Nanking under government auspices. He travelled extensively not only in China but also Burma, India, and Egypt. Ch'i-feng, the younger brother, who died eighteen years before Chien-fu, was given a state funeral by the Nationalist Government, a measure of the esteem in which the family was held.

The work of the Kao brothers and their Lingnan school received both praise and criticism in its day. Although they brought new subject matter into traditional painting, it is questionable whether the results can really be justified as new contemporary Chinese painting. The Western derivations behind the style came through Japan and were not always adequately explored, producing a hybrid result at best. In spite of this, the Lingnan movement had a considerable influence and left its mark on a good deal of Chinese painting. It was an experiment representative of its period.

While the traditional school of painting as personified by these men pursued its serene and unhurried way in the tumultuous years that followed the May Fourth Movement, there was a temporary rejection of the past on the part of some young painters. Among these was Hsü Pei-hung (1895–1953) from Kiangsu, one of the most brilliant and influential modern artists. He first learned the old-style painting from his father, a village schoolmaster-craftsman, and in his teens was already helping to support the family by teaching art in several schools. Later he went to try his luck in Shanghai, and in 1917 managed to go to Japan for some brief study. On his return he was given a post in the newly organised art department of Peking University whose talent-conscious chancellor, Ts'ai Yüan-p'ei, in 1919 recommended Hsü for a government scholarship to study in Paris. There he enrolled at L'Ecole des Beaux-Arts where he gained considerable distinction. He also spent a period studying in Berlin and finally returned to China in 1927 to be appointed professor of the new art department of the National Central University, Nanking. For a time he also directed the fine-arts section of T'ien Han's South China Society, then a centre for the intellectual bohemianism à l'Europe so fashionable among the younger generation. Hsü's arty appearance and authentic Paris background added a genuine touch to the Society.

But in 1929 the Paris bohemian discarded his left-bank attire for the Chinese gown, an outward symbol of a change in his work as he put down his palette and oils to take up the Chinese brush again. His painting now combined the free style of the Chinese brush and ink with a Western knowledge of anatomy and academic form. Typical were the studies of galloping horse that he painted at intervals throughout his career. The best of them were full of intense movement and vigour, although later they tended to become a formula. Chinese in conception, these prancing, snorting creatures demonstrated Hsü's grasp of Western academic draughtsmanship, although this was subordinated to the sheer native verve with which he handled his medium.

During the early thirties, Hsü's work caused great interest in Brussels where it was the first example of modern Chinese painting to be seen. In these years Hsü also accompanied a travelling exhibition of modern Chinese art to Paris, Brussels, and Moscow and renewed his acquaintance with the West again. By then he had become the presiding genius of the new movement propagated by his enthusiastic band of students in Nanking, and his artistic reputation was at its height. The war came, and after exhibiting in Indonesia and Malaya in aid of Chinese famine relief, Hsü went to India at the invitation of Rabindranath Tagore, of whom he did a portrait, and held two exhibitions. In 1942 he returned to Chungking to direct a

National Art Research Institute until the end of the war. In 1946 he became Director of the National Peking Art Academy, a post he retained until his death seven years later.

Hsü was a versatile and gifted artist with a natural dexterity in his chosen mediums. He covered a wide range of subjects and styles throughout his career—portraits and landscapes in the Western academic manner, figure drawings, animal studies, and large narrative compositions, in addition to a series of flower, tree, and bird studies in traditional Chinese style, and, of course, his famous horses. He probably had the most competent grasp of Western academic oil painting and draughtsmanship of any of the Chinese artists who adopted foreign techniques. Some of the large compositions with almost life-size figures that he painted between 1930–33 typify his mastery of Western academic treatment, although to an outsider there is little to distinguish them from hundreds of similar narrative canvases that were turned out as exercises in the academies of Europe during the first quarter of the century. In a later period Hsü attempted to combine large-scale Western narrative treatment with Chinese method and subject, but the results were artistically questionable.

Hsü's technical competence was in some ways an obstacle, for throughout his career he vacillated between Western and purely Chinese treatments. He was the product of a period that induced ambivalence in the Chinese artist. In the end his best work was probably achieved in a traditional genre, although as a product of the Beaux-Arts he was fated to try to solve his painting problems with the knowledge he had gained in Paris. If the school of painting that he fathered must be judged in retrospect on the grounds of technical rather than creative achievement, it must not be forgotten that both master and pupils were the children of an age whose artistic transition has still to be accomplished.

A parallel figure with Hsü Pei-hung in the modern

school is Liu Hai-su (1895–   ), also from Kiangsu. He was prominent in early art education and founded the Shanghai Art School in 1920. Liu studied in both Japan and Paris, and in contrast to Hsü Pei-hung's French academism became a devotee of the postimpressionist school. He admired Matisse, Van Gogh, and particularly Cézanne, whose technical influence was evident in a good deal of his work. In the late twenties he became involved in controversy because he engaged a nude model in his art school, an unheard-of thing in the China of those days. Liu soon abandoned Western techniques in his own work, but remained strongly influenced by them in many ways. His traditional brush-and-ink painting for a long time embodied elements of design and composition that owed more to French painters than to Chinese masters. Liu's better known pupils have followed orthodox paths, and he himself has now completely reverted to Chinese tradition. His later work shows the strong influence of the monk painter Shih T'ao (1630–c.1707) from whom the painter Chang Ta-ch'ien also learned a great deal.

The careers of the two talented men just described indicate better than anything else the uneasy technical truce that has existed from the start in the painting movement in modern China. In the long view, oil painting can only be regarded as temperamentally unsuitable for the Chinese artist. There seems little for him to say in the Western medium that cannot be said very much better in his own. And in view of contemporary Western painting developments, with their concentration on the abstract problems of art and "free" use of mediums, the Chinese artist need have no more inhibitions about it. He is better equipped in many ways to meet the artistic challenges than his Western contemporaries.

The work of men like Hsü Pei-hung and Liu Hai-su typified a phase of modern painting that was summarily ended by war. When full-scale fighting broke out in 1937, the government art schools, where the bulk of the modern artists were employed, evacuated to West China. Nothing very startling developed there in painting; teachers and students were engrossed in ensuring the bare existence of their institutions. Travelling exhibitions were organised, and some artists found a new outlet in recording the different tribespeoples of the West. But pure painting was chiefly confined to a nostalgic repetition of the past, or else it became the vehicle for a new realism depicting contemporary life in relation to the war. Propaganda became a dominant factor in painting as in other arts. Because of this, some of the more vigorous pictorial development was not in painting at all but in cartoons and woodcuts which can be more appropriately discussed under a new heading. Painting will be returned to later.

THE GRAPHIC ARTS

Wood-engraving

In 1929 a group of young Shanghai artists formed the Eighteen Society, so named because it was the eighteenth year of the Chinese Republic. Their slogan was "Out of the salons to the street corners" and their purpose a crusade against the "aristocratic arts." Art must be for the people, they said, and not just for the wealthy few, a precept that has tended to become a little stale with repetition in recent years but was revolutionary enough then.

The manifesto of the Eighteen Society impressed the writer Lu Hsün, especially since artists like Yeh Fu and Ch'en Yen-ch'iao were experimenting with wood-engraving, an art in which Lu Hsün had a lifelong interest. Wood-block printing in China was a finely developed craft with a history of about 1500 years, but the introduction of mechanical printing processes during the nineteenth century had caused a steady decline in the ancient methods, much to Lu Hsün's regret. His interest in wood-block printing led him to study Western prints by artist-engravers, a combination unknown to China where the artist and engraver were always two different persons, the latter regarded only as a skilled workman. Not only did Lu Hsün find Western artists' engravings technically superior as illustrations to the imperfect mechanical reproduction in China, he sensed the possibilities of the art as a quick and economical method of communication in the case of social revolution.

When the Eighteen Society held its first exhibition in the late spring of 1931, Lu Hsün was an enthusiastic sponsor, and he decided to encourage more young artists to take up wood-engraving. In August 1931 he engaged a Japanese instructor at his own expense and started a class with himself as interpreter. This study group emerged in 1932 as the Ch'un Ti Art Research Society and held its first exhibition in the early summer at the Chinese Y.M.C.A. After this the woodcut movement made considerable headway in Shanghai, and societies were founded in other cities. Throughout this period of development, Lu Hsün remained the father figure who gave freely of his time and money for the cause. Russian engravings of modern industrial construction so impressed him that he advised his young protégés to describe the realities of the present in their pictures. Their goal, he urged, should be a new and national art designed for the ordinary people, drawing upon the technical accomplishments of the West while retaining its Chinese spirit.

Under the circumstances, the new wood-engraving movement concentrated largely on social commentary. There was naturally a good deal of pure imitation of Western models and what one Chinese critic called a "predilection for tragic pessimism" which he felt should occasionally have given way to depicting the "positive facts" of contemporary life.

By the time war came in 1937, the numbers of wood-engravers had multiplied greatly. In 1938 the artists banded themselves together as the National Chinese

Woodcutters' Association at Wuhan from which they finally moved to Chungking. Their name was changed to the Chinese Wood Engraving Society in 1942 but reverted to the original title upon their return to Shanghai in 1945. In September 1945 they held a retrospective exhibition, entitled "Woodcuts of the Eight Years' War of Resistance." The exhibits covered the years 1937–45, and a representative selection was published in an album called *Woodcuts of Wartime China* published in 1946. *Fleeing Refugees, Calamity, Starvation, Consultation of the Farm House Programme, Repairing the Railway,* are a few random titles from the work of the hundred or so artists and suggest the nature of their work. Technically they followed well-trodden paths from a Western point of view and said little new artistically. As social commentary they tended to be repetitious, but here and there a print showed more adventurous exploration of decoration and design.

Two artists may be mentioned in passing for their historical importance in the development of the Chinese woodcut movement. There were literally hundreds of engravers at work, and most of their prints reached a standard of technical competence though they tended to be monotonous in artistic values, and it is difficult to pick out engravers who can be regarded as creatively original.

Yeh Fu from Chekiang, whose real name is Cheng Ch'eng-chih, was a student of the Shanghai Art Academy and a founder of the Eighteen Society which gained Lu Hsün's support. Yeh Fu worked unceasingly for the development of the wood-engraving movement in a number of ways. Early in the war he helped to found a co-operative enterprise for the manufacture of wood-engraving tools and so performed a useful service to artists. His own engraving, as exemplified by his print of fighting buffaloes in the 1946 exhibition, was conventional and broad in treatment. He was a promoter rather than a creative artist.

Ch'en Yen-ch'iao from Canton was a fellow student of Yeh Fu's whom he actively supported in the early thirties

[1] *Lao She the novelist and short story writer. Photographed at his home in Peking, 1956.*

阿Q遺像

[2] *Ah Q. Lu Hsün's famous character symbolising the ills of China. A brush drawing done by the artist Feng Tzu-k'ai in 1939.*

[3] *Lou the rat and the fortune teller. A scene from a famous 19th century Soochow play adapted and revived in Peking, 1956.*

[4] *A 1936 photograph of the Shanghai Tungnan Physical Training School girls practising in Broadway style.*

[5] *Miss Butterfly, China's most famous film star in the twenties. She is still making films in Hong Kong. A photograph taken in 1927.*

[6] *Pai Yang, the doyen of screen actresses in Peking today. She began making films in 1937. A photograph taken in 1956.*

[7] *Two characters from China's first cartoon film,* Princess Iron Fan, *made in 1941.*

[8] *Painting by Kao Chien-fu (1879-1951). The first attempt to use an aeroplane as a motif in a traditional style painting.*

Sketch at a Steel Plant   *Study in Chinese ink and colours by* **Ya Ming**

[9] *A contemporary painting of an industrial scene showing the freer interpretation of "social realism" possible with traditional technique.*

[10] *A Miao dancing girl. Contemporary woodcut by Huang Yung-yü.*

[11] *A strip from* Mr. Wang and Little Ch'en, *by Yeh Ch'ien-yü, one of China's best known cartoonists of the thirties and a pioneer in the genre. Mr. Wang is seen as an unsuccessful discus thrower and Little Ch'en as the cameraman. It is a comment on China's fashionable pre-occupation with Western sports in the period.*

[12] *Lamp standard in the T'ien An Square, Peking. The new National Museum is seen in the rear.*

[13] *Portrait bust of Mao Tse-tung* (TOP) *by the sculptor Liu K'ai-ch'ü. Statuary* (BOTTOM) *outside the new Agricultural Exhibition Hall, Peking. A communal work by students of the Lu Hsün Art Academy.*

[14] *A sing-song girl of 1912 photographed playing the harmonium, a fashionable studio prop of the period.*

KUANGLINGSAN

Music transcribed by Wang Ti
(based on Kuan Ping-hu's
rendering and interpretation)

[15] *An ancient composition,* Kuanglingsan, *for performance on the* chin. *Recently revived and here shown re-scored in Western notation.*

NATIONAL ANTHEM OF THE PEOPLE'S REPUBLIC OF CHINA

(March of the Volunteers)

Words by Tien Han
Music by Nieh Erh

[16] *The National Anthem adopted by Communist China in 1949.
The music was composed by Nieh Erh (1912-1935) and was first
used for a film theme-song in the thirties.*

during the initial stage of the engraving movement. He went to Hong Kong when war broke out and worked as a cartoonist; later he arrived in Chungking where he taught art for a time and did some writing, before leaving to travel in southwest China in search of materials. In many ways a more competent artist than Yeh Fu, Ch'en's prints are characterised by a precise treatment of white graving on black which makes them effective as illustrations, although they belong to a somewhat orthodox school.

The end of the war found many wood-engraving artists still committed to their social-realistic outlook, particularly as many of them had been in Yenan where wood-engraving was enthusiastically sponsored at the Lu Hsün Art Academy during the war years. The trend of post-war developments did nothing to change their outlook; if anything, it deepened the note of despair and tragedy that was echoed in their prints. There were a few who rose above their political dedication and sought a more poetical expression free from subservience to propaganda. An outstanding example is Huang Yung-yü (1924–) from Fenghuang, in Hunan. His father was a schoolmaster and his mother came from the Miao tribespeople whose folk art and customs have been a dominating influence in his work.

Huang had some painting instruction from his mother when he was a child, but he was largely self-taught as an artist after graduating from middle school. He has an exuberant personality bubbling over with enthusiasm for the life around him, and he is never happier than when he has his sketch pad in his hand. His youthful appearance is somewhat reminiscent of his own drawings of happy children, and people continually mistake his age. He was an elusive character to track down in the old days, and had the habit of changing the rented rooms he used as studios two or three times a month.

His *Miao Dancer*, exhibited at the Chinese Woodcutters' exhibition in Shanghai in 1947, gave the first promise of his maturing style as an engraver (see Plate 10). His best work has great lyrical quality, and all of it is characterised by an elf-like humour and an instinctive sense of decoration. He uses his gravers inventively, achieving bold patterns of black and white, and he has a fertile imagination.

In 1948 Huang went to Taiwan and later settled in Hong Kong where he held two exhibitions of his paintings, chiefly portraits and figure studies, particularly of Miao people, in which he used a decorative linear style vivid in its characterisation. These works emphasised the intensely personal and original quality of his vision, although the influence of artists like Modigliani and Lautrec was discernible in some of his paintings. In the mid-fifties Huang returned to China and now teaches wood-engraving at the Peking Academy of Fine Arts. His engraving, now very much in demand for book and magazine illustration, still displays his whimsical personality. He has had plenty of opportunity for roaming the countryside within recent years, for he has been on several "work and study" trips to different areas. But there is a certain hardness in some of his recent work that suggests the effects of prevailing artistic restraints on the mainland.

Cartoons

The Chinese artist's spontaneous use of brush and ink obviously provides the ready basis for a vigorous and original school of cartooning, although achievements in pictorial satire in twentieth-century China have been disappointingly meagre and often dull. One reason is the attitude of the Chinese themselves. The old-style intellectuals dismissed such an art as a "small means of cutting up insects," and in a society where losing "face" was the worst that could happen to a man, and social behaviour was designed to avert it at any cost, it was understandably an unrewarding occupation to debunk public men with drawings in the press. At no time within the last sixty years has the political situation been favourable for an uninhibited caricaturist, either under the monarchy, or the several leaderships that have replaced it in China.

After the 1911 Revolution there were sporadic attempts at political faction cartoons in the Chinese press, but they were mostly crude, poorly executed designs that did little to develop a sophisticated art of social commentary. It was Shanghai in its usual *avant-garde* role which first nurtured a competent school of cartoonists during the thirties when a number of new magazines appeared devoted exclusively to cartoons. These journals were aimed chiefly at the younger generation, and many of them had an ephemeral existence while others turned to eroticism and coarseness in their struggle for circulation and against the constant threat of political censorship. These circumstances, added to very low rates of pay, made satirical drawing even more a labour of love than usual for the aspiring cartoonist.

In spite of this some interesting work appeared during this period which, given more favourable conditions, might have initiated a tradition. Western influences were noticeably predominant among Chinese cartoonists and George Grosz, Covarrubias, Daniel R. Fitzpatrick, and David Low all had their imitators, but only one or two people struck out on original lines. Among these were two artists of widely different temperaments and outlook, Feng Tzu-k'ai and Yeh Ch'ien-yü.

Feng Tzu-k'ai (1898–), from Chekiang, was a pioneer teacher of Western art methods in Shanghai, and he lectured and wrote on the subject as well. He was a Buddhist and had studied Western painting and music in Japan, the goal of many Chinese students who could not get to Europe or the U.S.A. Feng worked in a number of teaching jobs and as editor for a publishing firm, but he first attracted public notice with his brush sketches done for reproduction in the Chinese press. A series of impressions of mischievous children, for many of which his own family were the models, first made him popular. They showed his knack of catching the essential spirit and poses of his subjects in their home environment. From these he turned to depicting the ordinary incidents of everyday life, such as a family in a station waiting room, or a young couple having their baggage examined by customs officers, and so on. Several collections of his sketches were published in book form. He used a bold and summary treatment dictated by his medium, and in his best drawings achieved a skilful economy of line and yet preserved vivid characterisation, as in the drawing of Ah Q (see Plate 2).

Feng was no satirist; he merely commented with a gentle smile on the foibles of human life that he saw around him. Many of his drawings were little more than hasty notes whose draughtsmanship was by no means always distinguished. But he has his place as one of the first artists to draw from direct observation with a Chinese brush for newspaper reproduction. Some of his sketches remain vivid thumbnail reminders of Shanghai Chinese society during the thirties.

Yeh Ch'ien-yü (1907–   ), also from Chekiang, is another kind of cartoonist altogether. Largely self-taught, he started his professional career in 1929 with drawings in the *Shanghai Sketch*, but leapt to fame with a strip cartoon entitled *Mr. Wang and Little Ch'en* (see Plate 11). Wang was the typical Chinese middle-class philistine and Ch'en his foil. Their antics appeared regularly in the pages of the *Shanghai Morning Post* and the *Nanking Post* where they delighted thousands of readers. The cartoons were done with a pen and showed great technical aplomb, being reminiscent of the style of the English cartoonist Gilbert Wilkinson. Looking back now, Mr. Wang bears a distinct likeness to Chiang Kai-shek although it obviously never struck anybody at the time—or if it did they kept quiet about it!

The Sino-Japanese War gave Chinese cartoonists a new importance and a freer hand with their satire—as long as it was directed at the right target. In August 1937, Yeh

Ch'ien-yü organised the first cartoonist propaganda corps, which began with eleven members and when Shanghai fell became a section of the Political Department of the Military Affairs Commission at Hankow. Here they produced a series of propaganda posters. Several by Yeh himself were highly successful examples of their kind. Later Yeh travelled a great deal as an official artist. He visited both India and the Miao tribal country in southwest China and did a series of impressions of peoples and places drawn directly from life with a Chinese brush, a technique he further developed later. In 1946 he was invited to the United States as a cultural visitor, although by then he

Cartoon of General MacArthur by Yeh Ch'ien-yü.

had already begun to abandon cartooning for Chinese painting. He returned to teach this subject at the Peking Academy of Fine Arts where he is today. A few cartoons from his brush appeared during the Korean campaign but he has given up cartooning again in favour of illustrations based on bold, free life sketches of figures done with the Chinese brush. His work appears frequently in the English-language magazines published in Peking.

Cartooning in Communist China has descended to pretty dull levels, and its one-sided attitude is merely boring. The hundreds of anti-American cartoons which are churned out monthly are, to say the least, technically second-rate. There is a certain amount of mild wit as in the comment on architectural extravagance on page 118 but there is no true satirical draughtsmanship with bite and polish. In a land whose leaders are immune from any form of honest portraiture there must obviously be less scope than usual for the great caricaturist.

THE CONTEMPORARY SCENE

After the Communists came to power in 1949, traditional painting was unfashionable and the Western style practised by the followers of the Paris school was under a cloud. At the All China Literary and Artistic Workers Congress held in July 1949, the Yenan spirit was invoked and artists were adjured to promote "Struggle and Construction," with woodcuts, broadsheets, cartoons, etc. Such Western-style painting as went on in this period consisted of heroic-figure compositions which, in the words of Kuo Mo-jo at the Second Congress in 1953, adopted "the precious forms of expression of Soviet Russia, the land of socialism." The official Soviet school of social realism has had a deadening effect on Chinese painting, but it has been closely imitated both in its technique and in its subject matter. The result has been a dreary outpouring of "revolutionary" compositions—portraits of leaders and official "subjects" whose laboured style is characterised by fictitious idealisation and a poverty of artistic content. The methods used are reminiscent of those favoured by the duller forms of Western painting sixty years ago.

At the October 1953 Second Congress of Literary and

Art Workers, traditional painting methods were restored to official grace with the blessing of Kuo Mo-jo who told his listeners that authors and artists having arrived at the stage of "planned construction" should seriously study the artistic heritage of their own people. The All China Artists' Union was re-organised and Ch'i Pai-shih, the old traditionalist, appointed Chairman of the Union to replace Hsü Pei-hung, who had recently died. But though traditional painting was back in favour, artists were urged to reflect reality in their work and there was a movement to introduce motifs like tractors, trains, and telegraph poles into traditionally rendered landscapes. This was an echo of the Cantonese painter Kao Chien-fu's ideas as far back as 1916, and his influence is apparent in certain Communist approaches to painting.

After 1953 there was a greater emphasis on full-scale figure compositions painted in traditional style, and here the influence of Hsü Pei-hung and his followers was visible. Instead of the tiny figures dwarfed by landscape that were characteristic of the old painting, soldiers, children, or peasants became the dominant pictorial element, invariably shown in that state of pictorial bliss that is one of the prerequisites of official inspiration.

By and large, the handling of the traditional-style paintings is fresher, livelier, and less heavy-handed than the overworked naturalistic conventions of the oil painters. Not that there is anything wrong with good illustration as such, and some of the better paintings in this class are interesting social records. But true painting is a private art, and it has little chance to be that in China at present and therefore little chance to achieve any spiritual depth.

In 1956, under a special government dispensation, free criticism against the regime was allowed, and the painters produced their crop of protests. One complaint was against a previous tendency to sneer at traditional painting. "In spite of everything, Chinese-style painters continue with their work," said a speaker at a meeting of the Peking Chinese Painters in the summer of 1956. And they *have* continued. If any style of painting can be regarded as in the ascendency today, it is one based on traditional methods. The official position towards the arts must be necessarily more complex in China than in Russia where there is only the one approved school of painting. And the Chinese traditional style offers a far greater range of freedom within prescribed subjects, as the painting of a steel plant (see Plate 9) shows. It is a straw in the wind which indicates new possibilities.

In the graphic arts, there is an ever-increasing army of woodcut artists, some of whose works may be seen regularly in English-language publications like *Peking Review* and *Chinese Literature*. The latter frequently publishes colour woodcuts which are now popular. Mostly landscapes, they are reminiscent of the work of first-year art students in Europe thirty or forty years ago. Among the dozens of black-and-white illustrations dealing with industrial and agricultural themes, an occasional print stands out as being concerned more with design than with propagandist reportage. Technically, there is much more experiment with printing and engraving than there was a few years ago.

The artist in China today has a basic security that he never before found in his profession. In addition to teaching, he is commissioned to do work for publishing and reproductions, for which there is a great demand, and on which he gets royalties. He is well paid by contemporary Chinese standards. His social standing is respected, and he is considered a necessity, not an outcast, in the new society. The fact that his artistic standards are defined for him is another matter altogether.

VI. ARCHITECTURE AND SCULPTURE

Architecture was never an independent profession in China in the past. The Chinese attitude towards any art was non-materialistic; architecture was therefore regarded not as an art but as a material necessity, an adjunct to the needs of daily living. Buildings were put up by masons and carpenters who in most cases simply followed written descriptions and material specifications. Only in a large project like a palace were any kind of plans required, and even these were only rough arrangements of layout.

Hu Shih, veteran of the May Fourth Movement, summed up the position of Chinese architecture when he wrote: "One of the questions which often puzzles the student of the history of Chinese art is why has China been deficient in certain arts while she excels in others? Why, for example, has China never achieved a higher level of development in architecture? . . . All ancient Chinese schools of thought unanimously condemned public expenditure on architectural grandeur. They praised the primitive simplicity of the houses wherein the legendary sage-rulers were supposed to have lived, and they taught that rulers who lavished the taxpayers' money on 'high roofs and curved walls' were destined to ruin their kingdom by extravagance. This almost universal condemnation was temporarily swept away during the long periods of domination by Buddhism and later Taoism. In the mediaeval period, wealthy and influential followers of both religions vied with each other in the building of temples and monasteries. . . . Orthodox Confucianist thought, however, continued to censure vast expenditures on either Imperial

Palaces or religious edifices. Because of this strong prejudice on the part of the scholarly class, China has produced no great architecture of the scientific and creative type. . . ."

This may appear harsh criticism to many people, and scores of reasons could be advanced to prove the greatness of Chinese architecture in ancient times—the skilful genius of its constructional principles and the nobility of its aesthetic rules which endured from generation to generation. But the core of Hu Shih's argument, that the historical evolution of Chinese architecture progressed little beyond what he called the "empirical crafts" of the master builder, mason, or carpenter, remains. While such builders accomplished constructional feats, they were restricted in their scope as creative designers.

Chinese architecture was primarily a matter of bricks and timber in structure, erected with supporting columns and beams. The mason and the carpenter were at a loss when it came to the problems posed by the buildings of an industrialised civilisation. Foundations, trusses, steel, and concrete materials demanded engineering knowledge beyond the experience of the old Chinese craftsmen. Appearance and effect were no longer related to the old structural forms, and the new "architects" could put up only inferior imitations of European styles.

The development of architecture in modern China divides itself into two main stages. The imitation of Western-style buildings, a method which has persisted through various phases until the present, and the attempt to create a new "national" style of architecture, which led to a movement that was somewhat euphemistically called the "Renaissance of Chinese architecture." Of the first stage there is little to be said. Western-style buildings in China meant those of a great trading centre like Shanghai whose indiscriminate mixture of styles and general lack of architectural unity was bound to lead Chinese imitators astray. Missionary Gothic and banker's international are a dubious source for inspiration at best. China today is covered with the architectural relics of the great age of European commercial expansion whose legacy of railway stations, ecclesiastical buildings, and commercial "palaces" in the modes of the nineteenth century is not a matter for artistic pride.

The movement to create a new "national" style of architecture was American-inspired and began with missionary organisations who sought to give local colour to their schools and hospitals by introducing Chinese design details in buildings whose basic construction was essentially non-Chinese. The "national" style was further developed by a number of young Chinese architects who had gone abroad for training, mostly to the United States where they absorbed the "Chinese" principles developed by American architects. It was not a creative movement at all although many people believed it was at the time, including, of course, the architects themselves. They returned to their country determined to do away with bad imitations of Western architecture and restore to life the glorious traditions of the past by adapting them to modern buildings. It was a mood well suited to that of the Nationalist Government, then in its most energetic phase and anxious to hasten national reconstruction in every sense of the word.

The movement was unsound, if only from its claims to be "national." To justify the title it would have been necessary to analyse traditional Chinese architectural form, a very different thing from decoration, and adapt it to methods fully in keeping with contemporary use of materials and techniques. The great qualities of architecture depend on structural values, and traditional Chinese styles had little to offer steel and concrete modernism except mere surface embellishment. The new "national" style merely accommodated stereotyped Western structure by grafting on Chinese design elements for outward effect. It was an Eastern equivalent of sham Gothic, fake Georgian, or any of the many bastard derivations that have passed for architecture since the Industrial Revolution in the West. The plans for a new Nanking railway station in 1930, for example, were supposedly inspired by the ancient Wu Gate in the Forbidden City. There could not be a more incongruous misinterpretation of the function of architectural design.

In the early development of the "national" style, architects went little further than using Chinese-style roofs. Typical examples were the missionary-run Nanking University and St. John's in Shanghai. The new *chinoiserie* was developed on more ambitious lines in buildings like Ginling Women's College, Nanking, and Yenching University, Peking, both completed in the twenties. In these institutions the facades of the buildings were treated with Chinese frieze and pillar decoration, while other touches here and there provided a suitable Chinese flavour to campus layout.

In an article written in 1937, a Chinese critic observed, "We had no quarrel with the tile roof on a Chinese temple, just as we have nothing to say by way of argument with such a consistent die-hard as Ku Hung-ming who kept his pigtail as a protest and a symbol. We would not object to a modern Gothic cathedral if built exactly as the mediaevals had constructed it in certain parts of Europe. It is perfectly sensible to erect a Buddhist temple, a tea pavilion, or a memorial hall with a tile roof, according to the classic Chinese formula and tradition; but it would be at once an anachronism and a fallacy if the tile roof is made to cover constructions of any size with a modern interior arrangement. . . ."

Yet this was what, in fact, was done all the time by the apostles of the new "national" movement. The traditional curved roof with glazed tiles has hypnotised foreigners ever since they first went to China, and certainly no one denies the grandeur and beauty of its construction in its original settings, like the Forbidden City in Peking. But its perpetuation in the twentieth century is an architectural affectation, as the critic emphasised. He went on to say: "In Tibet, Mongolia, Jehol, and particularly Kokonor, the combination of the tile roof and the terrace in one building has been typical for centuries. The surprise is that in this type of architecture the building looks as Chinese as the tile roof itself after the addition of a few windows and a simple coping on a plain wall. Most peculiar is the use of nothing but the flat roof, on one building after another, throughout many of the frontier regions; yet these buildings are astonishingly Chinese in appearance and have attained an artistic level such as those in the so-called Renaissance style can never reach. If this Renaissance style is going to survive, not merely as 'pigtail' architecture, it must reconcile itself to the flat roof. The burning question today, however, is not so much concerned with the flat roof as with the art of making it look Chinese. It would be illogical to adopt the Tibetan style, for the planning as well as the construction of a modern building is totally different. How to create a building in China, planned and constructed in the foreign way, with a native appearance is the problem taxing the brains of Chinese architects. The common practice is to treat the parapet with an open balustrade or in moulded coping in Chinese style. The elaborated carved base, characteristic of the palace building in Peking, is in most cases indispensable. There is little that one can do to the fenestration, save in the spandrel. As the building rises in height, windows become increasingly prominent and the Chinese characteristics at the top and base shrink into insignificance; on a tall structure such surface ornamentation is only skin deep. It has no true meaning other than mere sentiment, and little chance of being visible . . . at present classical Chinese architecture has nothing to offer to the modern building. . . ."

But not everyone was as perceptive as this in the first flush of enthusiasm for the new Chinese movement to which the Nationalist Government gave full support and encouragement. In 1926 there was a national competition for a design for Sun Yat-sen's memorial tomb to be erected on the slopes of the Purple Mountain, Nanking. The competition was won by a young architect, Lu Yen-chih, who was a graduate of Cornell and had studied the principles of "modern Chinese" architecture under its leading American exponent, who later became adviser to the Nationalist Government. Lu's design for the mausoleum was characterised by an ostentatious flight of steps and the ubiquitous Chinese roofing, while its proportions preserved an uneasy harmony with the landscape setting. It exemplified the pitfalls for the Chinese architect who found himself the trained exponent of a "national" style that was really synthetic. Lu died in 1928 before the work was completed, and it was taken over by his assistant, Poy G. Lee, who also completed Lu's designs for the Sun Yat-sen memorial auditorium in Canton.

Lee was born in New York in 1900 of Cantonese parents and studied at Massachusetts Institute of Technology and Columbia to become an architect registered in New York State. He went out to China for the Y.M.C.A. building bureau in 1923 and designed several hostels for them, as well as churches, quarantine stations, and schools in various Chinese cities. He was one of the several talented young men whose attempts to meet the architectural needs of their generation were influenced by the fact that their teachers were heirs to a tradition that stressed period detail at the expense of creative form. During the first thirty years of the century America still lagged behind Europe in architectural vision, in spite of her skyscrapers, whose size, as James Maude Richards has pointed out, was not an architectural virtue in itself. The only difference that marked the Woolworth Building from other "period" pieces was one of feet and inches. And so the new "Chinese" style was born in America at a time when that country's own national form of architectural expression was achieved in "pompous Classic" and "collegiate Gothic."

The transference of the Chinese capital from Peking to Nanking in 1928 heralded a period of intense re-constructional activities. A Chinese commission was sent on a world tour to select foreign advisers for the vast programme of building that was envisaged for public offices, not only in the new capital but in the various provincial and city governments as well. The new capital of Nanking was destined to become the unfinished monument to the Chinese architectural "Renaissance." In November 1928 a Nanking City Planning Bureau was organised and headed by Lin Yi-min, an American-trained engineer who was guided by two American advisers, Ernest P. Goodrich and H. K. Murphy, in their turn assisted by two more Americans, with W. Y. Cho as a Chinese chief of engineering and Y. Y. Wang as principal architectural assistant. Their task was to direct the building of Chiang Kai-shek's capital in the new "national" style. Two hundred public buildings were envisaged, thirty of them to house government departments, contained within a layout that it was thought would rival the Forbidden City in beauty and exceed it in area. The fact that a new Chinese capital in the twentieth century was thought of as a rival to the Forbidden City indicates the spirit that inspired the only really large-scale attempt at city planning and design in pre-war China.

The Nanking City Plan was completed within a year, and a six-year period of construction was put forward for a National Capital Reconstruction Committee to consider. But the plan was abandoned owing to political uncertainties, and a modified scheme was substituted. Even this was never completed, although some of the separate buildings to house various Ministries were begun. The first was the Ministry of Railways completed in 1930 and designed by Robert Fan and Shen Chao. It was the first public building to be erected in the new "national" style. The Museum for Party Relics, constructed during this period, was a faithful reproduction of ancient architectural style. The Ministry of Communications, built in 1934, was designed by a Russian architect. Building like this went on spasmodically until the war with Japan in 1937 finally stopped any further attempts at architectural developments in China.

Nanking in the post-war years presented a dismal picture. The few large buildings that had gone up in the thirties were scattered in shabby isolation through a ramshackle jumble of a city, whose principal saving grace lay in its beautiful natural surroundings. And even those were rapidly being despoiled by the ravages of the speculative builder. The one sign of "architectural" activity in the post-war capital was a rash of shoddily built Western-style houses and bungalows for which exploited foreign embassies paid extortionate prices.

When the Communists came to power in 1949, they inherited a negative architectural policy and a complex crop of problems. The years of war had left every major planning and constructional need in the country unfulfilled. The difficulties were enormous, and continue to be so. The Communists have tackled some of them with characteristic energy and startling results. The bridge over the Yangtze river is a case in point. It has been described as China's finest achievement in the first Five-Year Plan, although the Russian engineer, Konstantin Silin, must take a great share of the credit as the real genius behind the project and the inventor of a new method of sinking piers. Opened to traffic in October 1957, the bridge has a 3800-foot span over the water and is a double-decker with a six-lane traffic highway on the upper level and a double rail track below. A verse by Mao Tse-tung inscribed on a banner that floated over the girders on the opening day ran, "A bridge from North to South: an insuperable natural barrier becomes a thoroughfare." Certainly it is an engineering feat of the first magnitude, but as an example of architectural design it is open to some criticism, particularly in the eternal problem of combining Chinese and Western forms. The Chinese-style bridgehead pavilions are unsuitable in their setting, and the bridge itself has the nineteenth-century heaviness that is associated with so much Soviet design and, by implication, Chinese design today. In the matter of evolving a contemporary style the Communists have not yet proved any more successful than their predecessors, and in their Western-style architecture they have become imitators of Soviet neo-Communist classicism, at any rate in the public buildings of Peking which must be regarded as the architectural showpiece of the nation.

In a regime as bombastically nationalistic as the Communists were in their first year of power it was perhaps inevitable that immediate architectural instincts were to promote the "national" style in all its glory of glazed tile roofs and replicas of past greatness. An example was the Government Ceremonial Hall and Guest House in Chungking built between 1951–54. The central feature of this ornate construction was a replica of the Temple of Heaven in Peking, which dominated a building whose lavishness and cost were afterwards hotly criticised for their impractical extravagance. This came at the end of a period in which the apostles of the "national" style had been given a free hand.

In February 1955, the *People's Daily* (*Jen Min Jih Pao*) published a cartoon showing the Empress Dowager patting a present-day architect on the shoulder and saying: "You certainly know how to spend the money. I never thought of using glazed tiles for the kitchen when I built the Summer Palace." This marked the end of the architectural honeymoon with "curved roofs and high walls," which were now declared bourgeois in principle. Meetings were held by the Ministry of Building, and there was a spate of architects' confessions and repentances. Ideas were forced into line with prevailing Soviet dictates and a Moscow campaign to negate luxury and extravagance in public buildings.

So far as re-planning Peking went, the traditionalists never regained control. The many new buildings erected

since the mid-fifties are either unabashed imitations of Soviet styles pure and simple, or, if they do make concessions to Chinese traditions, use towers, the ubiquitous tiled roofing, superimposed columns, and replicas of the old-style brackets for staying eaves. The new Peking railway station is an example of this kind of mixture. The twin towers at the entrance are fussy and pointless, while the Chinese design elements are irrelevant to the general facade. The interior of the station drops all pretence of being Chinese, and the escalators, rest rooms, and waiting halls make it a far more spacious, efficient, and functional centre than the inadequate old terminus it replaced. But everything about the interior is redolent of the heavy hand of Soviet "classicism"—and this also applies to a majority of the new buildings, whatever their facades pretend to the contrary.

The new National Agricultural Exhibition Centre in Peking is an example of all that is worst in the attempt to blend sham tradition with imported ideas. The arrangement of the buildings is supposed to be reminiscent of Chinese garden layout, although the realistic and muscular group of statuary standing in the main approach to the Centre is imitative only of the monumental mason school of sculpture favoured in controlled societies. A description from a contemporary Chinese account gives the best clue to the real nature of the Exhibition Centre: "The General Agricultural Hall, around which the others are grouped, is particularly majestic. On its roof stand seven turrets glistening with green tiles and yellow walls. The broad granite steps in front of the entrance and the balustrades on either side are carved with designs of grapes, cotton bolls, and wheat ears. The floor of the main hall is red marble. Eight pink columns are capped with a fretwork of golden flowers. At the centre of the hall stands a large statue of Chairman Mao Tse-tung chatting with peasants, symbol of the flesh-and-blood relations between the Party and the peasants."

Other contemporary public buildings in Peking include the Centre for Returned Overseas Chinese, a dull construction in yellow brick and grey stone of a characterless kind to be found in any large city in the West, and the Chinese People's Revolutionary Army Museum, a blatant piece of second-hand Sovietism down to the last brick in the tower and the red star which surmounts it.

The use of heavily ornate lamp standards is a feature of all the new architecture in China. Those in the T'ien An Men, Peking, are typical (see Plate 12). Ostentatious and top-heavy in design, their chandelier form is sadly out of keeping with the spaciousness of their setting and the dominating pile of the old Imperial Gate, if well suited to the pillared facade of the Great Hall of the People flanking the square. The auditorium of this building which seats 10,000 is, incidentally, characteristic of the scale of architectural planning in contemporary China.

The *doyen* of the traditional school of architecture is Professor Liang Ssu-ch'eng (1901–), son of the famous Liang Ch'i-ch'ao, a prominent figure in the reform movement at the beginning of the century. Liang Ssu-ch'eng was educated at Pennsylvania and Harvard Universities. From 1931–46 he directed the Institute for Research into Chinese Architecture and led a number of field expeditions to study various styles and periods. He is regarded as the leading authority on his subject. An architectural historian rather than a creative artist, he is today Dean of the Architectural Department of Tsinghua University, Peking. He came under heavy criticism for his ideas in the early years of the regime, but made his peace with the Party in 1957. During 1961, a series of architectural forums held in Peking, Harbin, and Canton, focussed attention on the professor's theories again. In June of that year he was interviewed by the *Kuang Ming Daily* in Peking and made a long statement on architecture as an art.

Harping on the theme that architecture is the reflection of ideology, particularly class ideology, Liang climaxed a long exposition with the following precept: ". . . we should not criticise a building by divorcing it either from its historical background or from the needs of today. We should not, furthermore, take it apart and analyse each architectural element as if it were an independent thing. We should differentiate between heritage and tradition. The only criterion for analysis is what Chairman Mao has pointed out, political standards in the first place and artistic standards in the second place. . . ."

Soviet Russia's official attitude has been the condemnation of contemporary Western architecture as "modernism for modernism's sake." In determining what was most applicable to Soviet ideas, the classical styles of Greece and Rome were selected as fundamentally "civic" and therefore social in aspiration. Gothic and oriental architecture were coupled with mysticism and feudalism, while twentieth-century functional styles were regarded as the product of decadent capitalism. Such Russian "tail chasing" has posed some aesthetic problems in Peking which are reflected in three ways in the new Chinese architecture. First there is pure imitation of Soviet models; second, an uneasy fusing of Soviet and Chinese ideas; and third, a frank return to the pre-war "national" style as exemplified in the recently completed Peking Art Gallery.

Discussion of modern Chinese architecture inevitably centres round buildings of a monumental character, museums, administrative centres, and the like, by which the government sets such store and which have gone up at an astonishing pace. But when it comes to the matter of large-scale planning of housing and development, which by every logical deduction should be the dominating note of architectural progress under a "socialist" government, the picture is less impressive. It is true that housing problems in China are gigantic and cannot be compared with Europe in terms of sheer size, need for economy, and speed of construction. And the plain fact is that merely to have his own toilet is a sign of architectural progress to many a Chinese worker. There is not enough modern plant and machinery to go round; an ant-like human activity must still be the substitute for bulldozers and concrete mixers. Factors like these must be taken into account when making judgements about domestic architecture in China, and, considering all the difficulties, the construction that has gone on has been prodigious. Even so, that does not wholly explain away why projects that have been accomplished are so mediocre in architectural conception and design.

Whatever Marxist theory argues to the contrary, Europe presents the real example of modern architecture applied to an egalitarian society, and it is there that real progress in large-scale housing is being made. There are even signs that one or two East European countries, some of which made outstanding contributions to modern architecture in the past, are beginning to defy Soviet restraints. It is conceivable that Russia herself might be driven to outrival others in the field of modern architecture some-day, and that there will be a complete reversal of "aesthetic policy." If this happened, there could be imitative repercussions in China. But short of such changes, there seems to be nothing to veer her from what Professor Liang Ssu-ch'eng defines as "the Chinese and socialist new architectural style, which is what the people want and which has been put forward by the Communist party."

SCULPTURE

Sculpture in ancient China was primarily an art for the palace, the temple, or the tomb. The development of Chinese sculptural art was profoundly affected by the arrival of Buddhism which, through the founding of many temples and monasteries, encouraged the use of sculpture—particularly sculpture in the round. Until then Chinese sculpture had chiefly favoured low relief forms within stone panels, intended for the decoration of temples and tombs. Buddhist sculpture, which was naturally pre-eminently religious, found its first expression in rock caves whose interiors were carved with intricate series of figures. During the T'ang dynasty (618–906 A.D.), a golden age of artistic development in China's history, Buddhist sculpture reached its apogee of perfection in stone and bronze. Other notable products of this period were the charming terra-cotta figures of dancers, musicians, and mounted riders placed in tombs. They represented a more secular sculptural development of surpassing grace and vigour. The bas-reliefs of war chargers, emphasising the power and movement of the horse, were another favourite form of expression in those days.

By the time of the Ming dynasty (1368–1644 A.D.) Chinese sculpture was in a decline. Religious carving had lost much of its deep spiritual quality, and sculpture in the round was typified by the huge animal and human figures that lined the roads to the Imperial tombs in Peking and Nanking. They lacked the spirit and quality of earlier sculpture and were little more than monumental masons' copies of stereotyped patterns from the past.

During the Manchu period (1644–1911 A.D.) sculpture became a more or less forgotten art. The most accomplished techniques were found in the small-scale carving of ivory figurines of the Goddess of Mercy and intricate representations of houseboats and similar objects. Canton province was a great centre of ivory carving, and still is, for the craft has persisted into present times. During the heyday of the Manchu period some exquisite pieces of carving were turned out, although the craft gradually tended to specialise in trick effects at the expense of artistic purpose. A favourite feat was to carve one decorated ball within another, and this is still done. The Hong Kong shops are full of such pieces made to attract the tourist. Ivory carving has degenerated into a craft of overornamentation and endless repetition of the same forms. As a sculptural art it has very little creative to say.

Sculpture in whatever form it took in China was done by skilled workmen and master craftsmen whose work fulfilled certain religious or ceremonial needs, and who remained anonymous creators. It was not thought necessary to perpetuate their names, as it was painters'. Sculpture was not considered a fine art, and up to fifty years ago no Chinese would have regarded a sculptor as an independent artist as he was in the West. China had no Michelangelo.

In the years following the May Fourth Movement, when numbers of students were attracted to Western-style painting, there were a few who became interested in sculpture, although the Chinese who achieved any reputation in this medium were only a handful. Some of them managed to get to Paris, the artistic mecca for the modern East as well as the West, where they all became dedicated disciples of Beaux-Arts academism.

Because the Chinese were indifferent towards their own sculpture as an art, there were even less reasons for there being any knowledgeable appreciation of Western sculpture among them. The men who returned from Paris did not, therefore, face a very promising artistic future, apart from teaching others to follow in their footsteps. The better known of them secured occasional commissions for realistic celebrity portraits, or a decorative group in the civic statuary genre, but otherwise it was a limited field. There was no body of fellow sculptors with whom they could discuss their problems and compare notes. The sculptor was the outcast of the Chinese modern art world; he had little hope of constructive criticism or patrons endowed with the taste born of knowledge. Moreover, the architect, who should have been his closest ally, was, as we have seen, a man given to the practice of a retrograde art. The sculptor in consequence lacked any sense of direction.

Some of the leaders of the modern Chinese sculpture movement, if such a title can be applied to something that was never more than a by-product of the Shanghai studios, were to be found among a small group of men who had studied in Paris. Three important names were Liao Hsia-hsueh (1906–   ) from Yunnan, Hua T'ien-yu (1902–   ) from Kiangsu, and Wang Ling-i (1909–   ) from Shanghai. The last was a student of the painter Hsü Pei-hung, in whose old department he taught at the National Central University, Nanking, until 1948. All three of these sculptors studied at the Beaux-Arts, Paris. Among them Hua T'ien-yu possibly showed the greatest inclination to break away from rigid academic realism in favour of a more formalised decorative treatment of his medium.

But the veteran of all modern Chinese sculptors is Liu K'ai-ch'ü (1904–   ) who came from a peasant family in Kiangsu. He first studied traditional painting at the National Peking Art Academy where he graduated in 1927 and remained on as a teacher. The school was closed because of political disturbances, and Liu left for Nanking where his talents attracted the notice of Ts'ai Yüan-p'ei, that inveterate champion of the arts, by whose good offices Liu was eventually sent off to study in Paris. There he took up sculpture and made such progress that his teacher, Henri Bouchard, made him his assistant for two years. During this time he had the chance to meet men like Charles D. Despiau and Aristide Maillol with whom his master was friendly. Liu arrived back in China in 1934 and was appointed professor of sculpture at the Hangchow Academy of Fine Arts.

The style of Liu's work can be judged from some of his important commissions. They included a statue of Chiang Kai-shek for the Central Air Force Academy, a second of an air force martyr, Chao Fu-ming, and a memorial tower to the heroes of the Eighty-eighth Division who died in a famous battle against the Japanese. He also carried out an equestrian statue of a noted commander of the same division. His work can be described as "official" sculpture in every sense.

Liu spent the war years in Chungking and Chengtu, and after the war worked for the Shanghai Planning Bureau. Today he is Vice Chairman of the Chinese Artists' Union and Assistant Director of the Central Institute of Fine Arts, Peking. In 1955 he was one of several artists chosen to work on the reliefs of the Peoples' Heroes Monument in the T'ien An Men Square, Peking. He has done two portrait busts of Mao Tse-tung, the more recent of which was made in 1958 and is shown in Plate 13.

With such a tradition of academic realism behind them, Chinese sculptors had less trouble with the technical transition to meet party ethics than some of their painter colleagues. The academic sculptor has attained a new professional importance in China, if he has not exactly made artistic progress according to contemporary standards in the West. Communist governments are noted for their partiality to vast monumental groups celebrating the achievements of the proletariat in agriculture and industry, quite apart from the necessity of keeping a tangible image of the leader before the public eye on as large and repetitive a scale as possible. China is no exception to the rule, and productive workers, valiant soldiers, and happy peasants are modelled, carved, and cast with an energy that is equalled only by the enthusiasm with which hundreds of idealised and characterless portraits of Mao Tse-tung are made. Plate 13 shows a large ornamental group of statuary outside the General Agricultural Hall at the Exhibition Centre in Peking, a communal work made by the students of the Lu Hsün Art Academy. It is symptomatic of what goes on in contemporary China and emphasises a politically derived insensitivity among a people whose artistic strength has never lain in sculpture.

VII. MUSIC

Chinese music since 1911 has been dominated by a conflict between Western and traditional styles, much like the conflict in painting, although, generally speaking, music has been the more neglected art in modern China. The technical differences between Chinese and Western music are wide enough to make transition a complex problem demanding much research and experiment.

The most superficially noticeable features of traditional Chinese music are the use of an untempered scale and high-pitched, full-throated singing characterised by a falsetto technique developed on the stage where men played women's roles. But the differences from the West in approach go deeper than that, for the whole question of musical structure in China was related to the tonal basis of the Chinese language. Chinese is monosyllabic, and each monosyllable may be uttered in a level, rising, or falling tone, which affects the actual meanings of words and also forms the nucleus of independent musical composition, for each word has in its three tones the beginning of melodic movement. Language is therefore much more intimately related to melody in Chinese than in Western music. Tonal differences being integral elements of the actual word meant that Chinese musical composition was a more abstract process than the Western emotional equivalent. Because the tonal basis of language was so much a part of Chinese music it need not surprise us to know that the highest form of musical expression in ancient China was achieved in poems.

The musical quality of words being the foundation of

the melody in a composition meant that the choice of words, that is to say, their actual meaning, was determined only after the arrangement of melody and rhythm. Emotional quality was of secondary importance because a musical setting was created through the relationships of rising and falling tone lines, and this pattern was essential before all else.

The broad evolution of Chinese musical form was dependent on a system evolved for poetry, where the rising and falling tones were listed under one division, "oblique," and the even tone under a second division, "level," which contained a contrasting level element of three. Musical composition was constructed on the basis of these two tonal divisions, and each successive movement of tones in any work had to be one of the two divisions. The "oblique" represented positive qualities, and the "level" negative qualities; and rules of composition allowed the positive to be developed to varying heights and depth of movement, but the "level" remained at an average, although unrestrained as to pitch. Balance and order were essential to good composition and depended on the skilful arrangement of the elements described. This development of the music of poetry underlay the more important types of instrumental music such as that of the *chin* mentioned later.

Chinese notation was by means of characters derived from the names used for the degrees of the scale, and because of the historical evolution of scales there were several systems, none of them alike. During the Yuan dynasty (1260–1368 A.D.), a new scale roughly corresponding to the Western major diatonic scale was introduced into Chinese music, and this has largely persisted until modern times as the principal mode, although other modes have been used and were also used before Yuan times.

Timing, if it is shown at all in traditional notation, is merely a summary indication. The exact rhythm of performance is learned by ear as it is passed on from teacher to pupil on the basis of hallowed usage. In the old music-poem time was determined by the syllable as the controlling factor behind each line or phrase. In many forms the rhythm was left to the singer on the basis of the time dictated by the syllabic character of the poem.

This brief incursion into a few of the somewhat complex technicalities of ancient Chinese music may serve to show why the point of departure between the old and a new seemed so great to many younger Chinese after 1911. It resulted in their turning their backs completely on their traditional styles, and few of their early Western teachers had sufficient knowledge of or interest in Chinese music to bid them do otherwise.

Theatre music and the folk songs of the many provincial areas might have arbitrarily defined the two main categories of Chinese national music in the early years of this century, although both, in fact, were highly regionalised forms. China is a vast country of many provinces and minorities, each having its own musical tradition with strong local characteristics due to different dialects and customs. There is in consequence a colourful, expressive, and varied repertoire which was at that time largely unexplored by modern musicians.

Solo instrumental playing of a more sophisticated kind was principally confined to the *chin*, a type of lute with strings tuned to G, A, C, D, E, and the *p'i-p'a*, a pear-shaped lute with four strings tuned G, C, D, and lower G. The *chin* was played by scholars, who were the connoisseurs of its rather "highbrow" repertoire, and as a class of performers they dwindled steadily during the post-revolutionary years. The *p'i-p'a* in its turn had by then become mostly identified with the sing-song girl or the story-teller whose supersedence by modern types of entertainers, particularly in the former case, caused a decline in this instrument's popularity.

In the field of folk music, drums and percussion instruments were used a great deal. The technique of the drum beat with its interplay of tonal colour is a marked feature of the Chinese countryside, and one that has been particularly emphasised by the Communists within recent years. The bamboo flute is another instrument whose clear note is reminiscent of pastoral simplicity as in so many lands.

But while Chinese musical instruments served the individual purposes of the scholar, the actor, or the shepherd, there was no ensemble playing as we know it in the West, no concert playing for a large public audience, no great virtuoso demonstrating his art from town to town, no choral tradition, nothing with the depth and range of a grand piano, or the swelling rhythms of a symphony orchestra. The Western conception of music was just as puzzling (and ear splitting) to many a Chinese making an acquaintance with it for the first time as Chinese music was to a majority of Westerners.

The first step in Chinese musical transition therefore was the purely technical one of learning to play Western instruments or sing in Western style. Because missionaries were the earliest teachers of Western music in China, choral singing and harmonium playing occupied an important place in the elementary stages of Chinese instruction. In early Republican China the harmonium even became a symbol of the ultramodish at a time when everything Western was the rage. Plate 14 of a 1912 sing-song girl seated at one of these dreary instruments offers amusing proof.

The brass band was another Western importation that the Chinese adopted early and in curious ways. Presumably it first appeared in displays of imperialistic military pageantry rather than with the peaceful missionary. But until 1949 the brass band was commonly used in the funeral cortege of citizens of substance. The greater the substance, the more brass bands. Three were usual: one in front, another in the middle, and the third bringing up the rear of a procession. Airs as widely different as a hymn and a Sousa march were played simultaneously and out of key, at least to Western ears. The custom is still observed in Hong Kong.

Missionary education created a strong tradition of choral singing which has persisted in China to this day. Singing was also encouraged in Chinese government schools, particularly as it was possible to propagate nationalistic sentiment through patriotic songs. During the thirties, the government-sponsored Officers' Moral Endeavour Association encouraged military singing and maintained both a band and community chorus which gave regular concerts. Choirs and glee clubs were a feature of every missionary-run university, and the Y.M.C.A. introduced massed song recitals in Shanghai and other cities, a foretaste of something very popular in Communist China today.

Peking specialised in choirs. The one at Yenching University, a hundred singers strong, gave a performance of Handel's *Messiah* in the thirties. Haydn's *Creation* was performed at Nanking in 1936, largely by members of Ginling College for Girls and Nanking University, both missionary-run. Ginling College became famous for its music department, which turned out a number of competent pianists and vocalists. In Shanghai both Haydn's *Creation* and Bach's *Mass in B Minor* were performed by local societies during this period, and Chinese singers predominated on both occasions.

The first attempts at Western musical education in Chinese institutions were in art schools or art departments of certain colleges. An early one was the Shanghai Art School, re-organised by the painter Liu Hai-su in 1920, which first included music as a full curriculum subject in 1925. In 1918 the Peking Normal College under Ts'ai Yüan-p'ei opened a department of fine arts which added an institute of music in 1925. This was closed when the fine arts department amalgamated with Peking University in 1927 and the government established a National Conservatory of Music in Shanghai, of which Ts'ai Yüan-p'ei was honorary director and Hsiao Yu-mei the principal. The first enrolment took place in 1927 when twenty-seven students were admitted.

Hsiao Yu-mei (1884–1940) was a Cantonese, a graduate of Tokyo University and Leipzig Music Academy, and a specialist in the theory of composition. He held various educational posts before being appointed to the Conservatory, which he directed until the outbreak of war in 1937. He did a great deal of research into the problem that worried all Chinese composers of the period—how to write the words for the music, whether to retain the old rhyming rules of classical Chinese or to break away completely in favour of ordinary speech. A common solution was the use of alternating long and short lines used in a rhyme appropriate to the content of the words.

Hsiao Yu-mei wrote a number of songs to demonstrate his theories. A famous one was "Willow Catkin," first published by the Commercial Press in 1930, with words by I Wei-chai. Another well-known work was his piano arrangement for the orchestral composition *New Chinese Ballet* published in the same year.

Under Hsiao's direction the Conservatory expanded rapidly; enrolment doubled within the first year and the school twice had to move to larger premises. Courses were run on a credit system, one hundred being required to complete a professional training course. In October 1929 the vocal training section was taken over by a Chinese woman instructor, Madame S. M. Wu. Composition was taught by Huang Tzu, piano instruction was in charge of a Russian. A cello class was started in 1930 under another Russian, and violin was taught by an Italian.

The Ministry of Education requested some changes in the course system in 1930, and a normal course was added to the academic course in which eighty credits were stipulated for any subject. In 1935 an organ class was added to the curriculum, and three new Chinese professors with European training were appointed, including Hsiao Shu-hsien, the niece of the director and a specialist in counterpoint. In the same year the fixed-*do* system was officially adopted by the Conservatory. By 1937 the official enrolment was one hundred and ten students, of whom a half were studying piano, a third taking vocal training, and the remainder learning violin or cello, with two solitary students studying the Chinese lute.

The Conservatory's vocal training programme was enhanced by the fact that several of China's most promising song composers were on the staff. Chao Yüan-jen was one of them. His collection, *Songs of Contemporary Chinese Poems*, published in July 1928, included well-known pieces like "Autumn Bell," "Listening to the Rain," and "The Drinking Song." But among all the staff members Huang Tzu (1904–38) was the most famous and remains probably the best remembered name in modern Chinese musical history. He came from Kiangsu and studied the piano in Shanghai under a Chinese teacher, Ho Lin-i. In 1925 he went to the United States and studied music at Yale University. On his return to China he taught first at Shanghai University and then at the Conservatory where he became responsible for training every well-known musician of his era in theory and composition.

His collection of songs published in 1933, which included "Spring Thoughts," "Thoughts of Home," and "Red Rose Three Wishes," will be recalled with nostalgia by many Chinese music lovers of a perhaps more sentimental era. Huang Tzu made a study of folk songs and experimented with adaptations. A major work, unfinished at the time of his death, was an opera-style song in ten movements, three of which were never completed, "The Tragedy of the Imperial Concubine Yang Kuei-fei."

During the early years of the Sino-Japanese War he composed two morale-raising songs which became famous, "Fight against the Enemy" and the "Army Flag Song." He was also the composer of the music for the National Anthem of the Republic of China. His early death from paratyphoid was a great blow to music circles in China.

When the Japanese war spread in 1937, the Shanghai Conservatory was unable to evacuate because of its foreign staff problems, and it was taken over by the Nanking puppet government in 1942. But in 1943, former teachers and students founded a "branch" conservatory in Chungking where the Nationalist Government had already founded a new National Conservatory in 1940. The latter moved back to Nanking after the war, while the branch conservatory returned to Shanghai to re-establish the old institution as the National Shanghai Conservatory.

While academic training of the kind described above was creating a knowledge and appreciation of serious Western-style music among the Chinese, there were other and more popular forces at work conditioning the public's ear to the rhythms and melodies of the foreigner. The radio, the cinema, and the gramophone were important influences, and the popularity of Western ballroom dancing in Shanghai introduced jazz forms to a sophisticated younger set. The Chinese were not long in assimilating such influences and creating their own popular sentimental style which was nicknamed "yellow music." It spread like wildfire through the dance halls and provided the films with many "hit songs."

The king of "yellow music" makers during the thirties was Li Chin-hui, who was defended as follows by a Chinese writer, Wen Yüan-ming, in a 1934 article: ". . . a writer of popular songs, he has been called charlatan, impostor, and immoral. From the very beginning of his career until today he was shunned by society as a person vulgar and depraved beyond the hope of redemption. He has not only written songs that appeal especially to maidservants and cabaret girls, but has also had the bad taste to allow his wife and daughter to see the girl choruses trained by him. . . . Musicians have heaped abuse on Mr. Li and have found faults with his compositions, but in spite of all this Mr. Li is as popular as ever. Although he employs the technique of Western music, his tunes are essentially Chinese. He is not content with copying others, that is why he is called an upstart by other musicians in China."

It was Li Chin-hui who, in 1931, signed up a young musician called Nieh Tzu-yi in his Bright Moon Variety Company. This beginner later became known as Nieh Erh whom the Communists have immortalised as a national composer. Nieh Erh (1912–35) was brought up by his widowed mother in Yunnan and learned to play the violin at the Kunming Provincial Normal School. His job with the Bright Moon Variety Company was his first paid professional employment, and from it he got a contract with the Lien Hua Film Company in Shanghai. Between 1932 and 1935 he composed more than thirty songs, mostly for films, many of them very popular at the time. During his work for films he collaborated a good deal with T'ien Han, who wrote many of the lyrics Nieh Erh set to music. Moving as he did in the progressive intellectual-artistic circles of the period, Nieh Erh decided to join the Communist party in 1933. In 1935 he was forced to take refuge in Japan, where he was drowned while bathing at Kuganuma, a tragic end to a talented young man.

Nieh Erh's greatest claim to musical fame is the music he composed for a poem written in 1932 by T'ien Han, called "The March of the Volunteers." It was first used as a theme song in the film *Children of the Storm,* and opens with the stirring injunction "Arise all you who refuse to be slaves. . . ." It became very popular during the war as a patriotic melody, and in 1949 the new Communist Government proclaimed it the official national anthem of China (see Plate 16).

It is no slur on Nieh Erh to say that he is lionised disproportionately today, and more because he was politically persecuted than because he was a musician of the top rank. He had a natural talent and created songs charged with the sincerity of his own youthful emotions, but he was too inexperienced to be hailed as a great composer. He himself would have readily admitted that he needed further training and study to become a finished artist.

The name of Nieh Erh is automatically coupled with that of the composer Hsien Hsing-hai in present-day China, where the two men are looked upon as "pioneers of proletarian music." Hsien Hsing-hai (1905–45) was the son of a Cantonese boat worker who died leaving his child to be brought up by its peasant mother. She emigrated to Malaya, and here Hsien received his early education. He returned to Canton in 1918 and by dint of working at various jobs managed to study in the music departments of both Lingnan and Peking Universities, where he specialised in violin and theory of composition. In 1927 he enrolled at the new Conservatory in Shanghai but was expelled because of his political affiliations. In 1930 he managed to get to Paris through the sponsorship of the composer-violinist Ma Szu-ts'ung, and he continued his musical studies under teachers like Vincent d'Indy and Paul Dukas.

Returning to China in 1935, Hsien worked for two different film companies and composed a number of songs. He also started work on a symphony. At the outbreak of the Japanese war he engaged in patriotic propaganda campaigns and finally, in 1938, arrived at Communist headquarters in Yenan where he was made director of the music department of the Lu Hsün Art Academy. In 1939 he composed his *Production Cantata*, a combination of song, dance, and drama drawing heavily on folk sources. In 1940 he went to Russia to continue his studies. There he completed his *National Symphony*, begun in 1936, and composed his second symphony entitled *War in a Noble Cause*. In 1945 he died of tuberculosis in a Moscow hospital without ever having been back to China.

His *Second Symphony* was given its first performance in China in 1960 by the Students Orchestra of the Central Conservatory of Music in Peking, where it was hailed as an important musical event. The work is in one movement with a theme based on the "Internationale" and offset by a conflicting motif of two rhythmic sextolet accentuated phrases. A Communist critic described it as follows: "Hsien Hsing-hai had a great talent for the creation of musical imagery. This is well exemplified in his use of the theme from the 'Internationale.' The first variation of this evokes an image of peaceful Soviet life and labour, an idyllic picture. When it reappears as a counter theme to that of the Nazis, the effect of rapid figuration with the use of dotted rhythm infuses it with a sense of mighty power throbbing beneath the anger of the people. The variant that follows immediately, with its rapid passage begun with syncopation, gives a vivid picture of the people rising in their might. Towards the end the theme surges forward again like a rising tide, a call to advance. Hsien Hsing-hai's use of this theme is an excellent example of his realistic and programmatic method of composition."

This is perhaps as good a commentary as any on the nature of modern Chinese music, and the criticism it inspires.

Ma Szu-ts'ung, mentioned earlier as a sponsor of Hsien Hsing-hai, is one of the outstanding violin performers in China. Also a Cantonese, he went abroad at an early age and received an academic musical training in Paris where he distinguished himself in his particular field. He returned to China in 1929 and became active in musical education, teaching in Lingnan University and the Central University in Nanking where he organised the first Chinese Symphony Orchestra. He also ran his own academy in Canton. Between 1929 and 1949 he composed many songs inspired by his study of folk music. "Song of a Shepherd," "Tibetan Song," and the choral works, "All the People Sing" and "In Spring Everyone Sings" were typical. During the war he travelled around giving concerts under government auspices. He is now director of the Central Conservatory of Music in Peking.

The war gave an impetus to the Chinese love of mass

choral singing, and there was an outbreak of spirited marches and patriotic tunes designed as morale boosters for both troops and civilians. Nieh Erh's "March of the Volunteers" has been mentioned; there was another piece, written by Lo Chia-lun, the Chancellor of National Central University, and set to music by Huang Tzu, called "Military March." Its most famous lines are:

> . . . charge through Shanhaikwan
> Redress our humiliations at Shenyang . . .

and it is typical of many songs sung by a Travelling Chorus founded in 1939 under government auspices. The members were mostly ex-Shanghai Conservatory students and teachers who spent their time travelling around West China giving concerts to aid the war effort.

The nature of wartime musical needs induced increased interest in the songs and music of the country areas, and there was a good deal of experiment and adaptation, particularly in the Communist-controlled areas where this type of music was extolled above all other forms. But the general theme of all wartime music, whether it was the marching songs of the troops, student songs, chanted recitative, operas, or orchestral pieces, was the nation's struggle against the Japanese invaders. Patriotism and propaganda prevailed.

After the war attempts were made to direct musical activities back into channels of new development. The Conservatories at Nanking and Shanghai returned to their old homes, and teaching began again under innumerable handicaps. The Nanking Conservatory was particularly short of equipment and too soon became pervaded by the attitude of despair that grew within all educational institutions in the last desperate years before the Nationalist Government collapsed. The Chinese Symphony Orchestra began its concerts in the Music Bowl in Nanking and was constantly handicapped by a lack of string players. Vocal and piano recitals by the better-known Chinese pianists and singers were given from time to time. Ginling College in Nanking was particularly active in sponsoring piano recitals, but concerts were all too few in proportion to the numbers who wished to hear them.

In 1948 a recital of Chinese music was held in Nanking under the sponsorship of the British Council for Cultural Relations office. The performers were two experts from the Conservatory, one a leading exponent of the *erh-hu*, a bowed, stringed instrument whose softer tone has caused it to be nicknamed the Chinese "violin," and the other a master of the *p'i-p'a*. The recital was the first of its kind in Nanking and was attended by a large and interested Western audience. It was intended to inaugurate a new phase of Chinese musical demonstrations, but political events prevented further experiment.

The various national cultural relations' organisations in post-war China attempted to remedy musical deficiencies in a small way by holding concerts of recorded music. The United States Information Service and the British Council were particularly active in this way. The author was responsible for the British activities in Nanking during 1947–49, and one of the clearest impressions that comes down from that now curiously unreal period is one of rapt students listening to some loved classic.

In the British case it was an unequal struggle to promote programmes of composers like Britten, Bax, or Walton as a variation from Tchaikovsky and Beethoven. The students listened politely and always came back for more —Tchaikovsky and Beethoven. These were the only two Western composers that existed for a majority of Chinese students, and, judging by recent musical events on the mainland, the situation is not markedly changed.

The development and expansion of radio after the war meant that "yellow music" attained a new era of popularity in those troubled years. Perversely enough, one of the most popular pieces trilled by the cabaret girls of the period was "Dream of Spring," a tune which had been the most popular among the occupying Japanese troops during the war under the title "China Night," and was said to have made them so homesick that it was finally forbidden. Whether or not that was true, new words to the old setting made it equally as popular in post-war China.

Oh, I can never forget that spring dream!
Already the snow on the mountains was melting
The ice in the stream was thawed by the spring winds,
We met again by the side of the river,
Then I awoke, aiya, aiya!
What a terrible thing it was only a dream
An unforgettable dream.

It was unforgettable in less sentimental ways, for one of the trials arising from radio was the installation of public loud-speaker systems throughout the main streets of Nanking. During the day the music of military bands, symphony orchestras, and the songs of the cabaret girls blared forth in an insensitive cacophony of sound, inter-mingled with moral exhortations and pep talks from Nationalist headquarters—a technique that has been considerably improved upon by the Communists who, in this as in a number of fields, have merely taken over where others left off. The love of massed choral effects, for example, so popular in Peking today may be inspired by Soviet Army Ensembles and Cossack Choirs, but a passion for large-scale vocal performance is not new to China, and can be traced back to the missionaries' zeal.

The post-war musical trends that have been so lightly touched on here were but drops in an ocean of national deficiencies. Any serious musical development in this period was severely handicapped by financial deficiencies and the chaos of the social scene in general. No one looking back could say that there was much more than a general marking of time on the situation as it had been in the musical world before the war.

THE CONTEMPORARY SCENE

The Communists took over China to the accompaniment of song and dance, the simple and sometimes primitive melodies and steps of the countryside. But there were new songs, too, which, while they followed well-tried metrical forms, proclaimed a note of social sentiment and class consciousness in their words. One most often heard as students and school children paraded the streets was:

> Red the sun rises in the East
> China has brought forth a Mao Tse-tung,
> He works for the welfare of the people
> Ai ya yo he is the peoples' great benefactor. . . .

For a short time songs like this mingled with the old "yellow music" airs, but these were gradually heard less and then suddenly disappeared into the disreputable past that a new order now denigrated in songs with a fashionable political theme.

Once the first phase of revolutionary conquest was over, music and musical training began to receive serious attention in Communist China. Since those early years there have been extensive developments in both Western and traditional instrumental and vocal performance. Research into and revival of old forms has gone on; so has the adaptation of traditional styles to new purposes. But not all the results are admirable as musical art.

The emotive nature of music makes it a vital medium for any revolutionary cause, and China's rich background of peasant music provides a ready-made basis for developing an "official proletarian" music, just as the local dramatic forms do in the theatre. The fad for "folk" music has produced quantities of songs and compositions affecting a pseudo-popular idiom and confusing a genuine creative musical culture with politico-ethnic description. Such artificiality is invariably supported by the formation of the amateur choruses and ensembles so beloved of Communist countries. Their numerical strength is held up as proof of spontaneous artistic development, when frequently it is the result of a kind of cultural drill system. In China's Western-style music, too, worship of the folklore fetish is reinforced by a debasement of values which make music an illustrative medium for imitating situations and events in the sterile manner of Soviet-inspired "social realism." Nevertheless, these harsh strictures do not preclude recognition of much useful work that has been done in the technical development of Western-style music in China, as well as a vast amount of valuable research that has been carried on in the case of traditional music in both its classic and "folk" forms.

Enough has already been said about Communist China's two most famous composers in the Western genre to make it clear that she has not yet advanced much beyond the gropings of other days in the field of creative composition. And as long as a work like Beethoven's *Ninth Symphony* is described as having "its call for solidarity of people the world over in their dauntless march towards freedom, equality, and a happy life, expressing the heartfelt wish of the people of China today," there can be little real progress in musical composition.

The words quoted were written in 1959 by a Communist critic, when the work in question was performed in Peking by the Central Philharmonic Orchestra supported by the Central Radio Choir. It was a musical highlight in present-day China and commemorated the tenth anniversary of the regime. The performance was given by ninety-three musicians and one hundred and forty singers led by the baton of a thirty-seven-year-old conductor, Yen Liang-kun.

Besides this orchestra there are in Peking the Central Broadcasting Symphony Orchestra, whose name speaks for itself, and the Orchestra of the Central Newsreel and Documentary Film Studio, which gives public concerts of which there has been a noticeable increase during 1961–62, now that a greater flow of trained musicians is becoming available from the academies.

Recent performances by the orchestras named will serve to give some idea of the type of programmes given within the last two years. The Broadcasting Symphony Orchestra gave a concert consisting of Rossini's *Barber of Seville* overture, Beethoven's *Violin Concerto in D Major*, and Dvořák's *New World Symphony*. The same orchestra also accompanied a recital by Chu Chung-mo, a tenor, who sang arias by Mozart, Schumann, and Tchaikovsky as supplements to "The Immortals," a poem by Mao Tse-tung set to music for vocal performance. The Central Newsreel and Documentary Film Studio Orchestra at about the same time gave a concert consisting of Weber's *Der Freischütz* overture, Beethoven's *Sixth Symphony*, Mozart's overture to *Cosi fan tutte* and *Eine Kleine Nachtmusik*. In December 1961 there was a special occasion when the Central Philharmonic Orchestra performed under a guest conductor, Anosov of the Soviet State Symphony Orchestra. Tchaikovsky's *Fourth Symphony* was given, and, according to critics, it was the best performance of the orchestra to date. The same programme included *Song of the Forest*, a tone poem by the Chinese violinist-composer Ma Szu-ts'ung.

The Central Philharmonic Orchestra was founded in 1956 and since then has given hundreds of performances throughout China. For the first two years of its existence the orchestra had a Czech conductor. Its repertoire of Western classics included Beethoven's *Third* and *Fifth Symphonies*, the Chorale from the *Ninth*, Tchaikovsky's *Fifth* and *Sixth Symphonies*, Dvořák's *New World Symphony*, Shostakovitch's *Fifth* and *Eleventh Symphonies*, and Prokofiev's *Seventh*. Selections from Mozart's *Requiem* have also been performed. There are two resident conductors, Li Teh-lun and Yen Liang-kun, who have both studied in the Moscow Conservatoire under N. P. Anosov and V. G. Sokolov. Li was conductor of the Yenan Central Orchestra from 1946–49 and accompanied David Oistrakh, the violinist, when he toured China in 1957. There are some two hundred musicians and singers, including Liang Mei-chen, soprano, and Wei Chi-hsien, baritone, who were the principal singers in the performance of Beethoven's *Ninth* Chorale already described. The Central Philharmonic has performed in collaboration with a number of distinguished foreign groups and individual artists, including Oistrakh, the pianists Serebryakov and Nicolayeva, the Soviet State Symphony Orchestra, the Dresden Symphony Orchestra, and the Ballet Rambert. The majority of the members of the Central Philharmonic are young—their average age is below thirty—and received their training at the various national conservatories.

Besides the orchestras performing Western-style music there are a number of traditional instrument ensembles for the performance of classical Chinese music and folk music. The Central National Music Ensemble is the largest of these. It grew out of the Central Song and Dance Ensemble, an orchestra and a folk chorus of twenty girl singers founded in 1952. The new ensemble has eighty players, all experienced performers on various traditional instruments. The Central Peoples' Broadcasting Station runs a similar orchestra for traditional music.

The principal musical education centre in China is the Central Conservatory of Music in Peking, founded in 1949 to replace the old Nanking National Conservatory, and under the direction of Ma Szu-ts'ung, the violinist. The Conservatory has seven main teaching departments: composition, conducting, symphony, vocal, theory-history, pianoforte, and Chinese classical-folk music. All students are boarders, and entrance requirements are high, with stiff competition for places. Tuition and residence are free with a monthly charge for food. The school has an extensive library and a record collection running into tens of thousands of discs. Attached to the Conservatory are a primary and a middle school open to children who show musical aptitude and want to train for admission to the parent academy.

There are other conservatories, in Shanghai (a successor to the old Academy), Tientsin, Chungking, and Mukden, while Canton and Sian have music schools. There is also a Research Institute of Chinese Music in Peking, which carries on a systematic study of both the music and instruments of the classic and folk traditions. Folk music has a wide variety of styles—songs, ballads, dances and instrumental music—and a great deal of interesting material has come to light during the research and recording which has gone on in the different areas.

A very special feature of Chinese folk song is the kind of chants and choruses used by peasants or labourers at work. They may be ploughing, planting rice, building a house, or hauling on a rope; they may be women working in the fields or plaiting bamboo straw; whatever kind of labour it is there will certainly be singing to accompany it. It is not so much singing for singing's sake as a rhythmical accompaniment to the tempo of the task in hand. Often there is a leader whom the chorus follows. This music has a practical purpose; besides regulating the progress of the labour it exhilarates the workers and lessens their fatigue.

Love songs, sometimes sad and melancholy, sometimes gay avowals, are another characteristic feature of local traditions and show a freedom from the more cloistered attitudes surrounding the ladies of the city. The feudal marriage system also inspired a good deal of song that often portrays "the course of true love" protesting or defiant against the shackles of forced marriage.

In many cases these songs are sung unaccompanied. Sometimes groups of performers sing antiphonally, and on occasion, as with the work songs, there is a leader and a chorus. Chinese folk singing is generally high pitched with the natural voice blending into falsetto. Common rhythms are a strongly accented $\frac{2}{4}$ or $\frac{4}{4}$ and alternating $\frac{3}{4}$ and $\frac{6}{8}$. A characteristic melody has a lively stepped form in the pentatonic scale with leaps of a fourth or even an interval. *Fa* and *te* in the scale may be sharp or flat, often in that order.

Thousands of these folk songs have been collated from different areas during recent years, and many of them have been incorporated into the repertoires of the various song and dance troupes that travel the country and tour abroad. Nor unexpectedly there has also been a spate of new "folk" songs, praising the Red Army, revolutionary heroes, the Communist party, production, industry, and, of course, Chairman Mao. In some cases new words are set to old tunes, or old tunes changed to suit a Westernised harmony. Other songs are merely synthetic imitations of traditional forms. For instance, in 1958, the year of the "Big Leap," the whole nation was set to composing new folk songs at the call of the Party. According to official statistics nearly a million newly "composed" songs were collected by the end of the year. Chou Yang, the supreme Party spokesman, a man who never did anything creative in his life but whose word is law on all matters of art and literature, praised these "creations of the masses" as the poetry of the new era. Most of the songs imitated the hallowed style of the old folk song—verses of four or eight lines with five or seven characters to the line—and that was as far as they got towards being either poetry or folk song. One Party critic expressed the feeling of a good many when he protested that he would "rather listen to the singing of the summer cicadas in front of a window than be invited to be a judge of such poems." The one consolation is that dross like this disappears with time, and there is ample proof in the folk music of China today that much gold remains.

Along with the attention paid to folk music within recent years has gone a revival of interest in the old classical styles of music and the instruments used. The *chin,* one of China's most ancient stringed instruments, in particular has received a new lease of life. The *chin* is played horizontally on a table, the seated performer plucking the strings with both hands; it is about 1.2 metres long and does not have a large sound volume. An old writer likened a famous work for the *chin* to "the sound of precious stones falling on a jade tray," which is typical of the descriptive terminology of the traditional Chinese critic. On the whole the repertoire of the *chin* is enjoyed by the connoisseur rather than the "lowbrow."

Twenty-five centuries ago the *chin* was used for sacrificial and ceremonial purposes. A knowledge of its technique was regarded as necessary to the Confucian scholar, the superior man, who was exhorted to achieve a cultural "wholeness" through music. In later centuries the instrument lost a great deal of its ritual significance as new music was written for it. By the time of the Ming dynasty (1368–1644) there was a large repertoire of both solo pieces and songs to be sung to the accompaniment of the *chin*, around which an extensive literature grew up. The *chin* had a new vogue, and various schools of playing which had developed through the years reached a peak of critical appraisal and method. Towards the end of this era some schools gave full support to the belief that the *chin* was intended purely for solo instrumental purposes and not for voice accompaniment.

After the Ming dynasty *chin* music became more and more the limited preserve of the few. During the Manchu times its popularity steadily waned, until by 1911 it was almost a dying art. A few attempts were made to bring about a revival during the Republican era, but the exponents of this ancient instrument had become limited in number and it remained at best the hobby of small groups of enthusiasts. By 1949 there were only a few experts left, scattered throughout the country, to uphold the ancient traditions of *chin* playing.

In 1954 the Central Conservatory of Music in Peking

started an Institute for Research into Traditional Chinese Music and a special department was formed to study the *chin*. Veteran performers were contacted and study groups were organised for younger musicians. In 1956 Ch'a Fu-hsi, a seventy-year-old specialist in *chin* playing, was sent with a team to travel round and search out old scores and manuscripts, and make recordings of performers in the various provincial areas. As the result of these investigations about one hundred ancient melodies were said to have been recorded and more than two hundred collected. The result has been an increased knowledge of the old pieces, many of which have now been transcribed for performance.

One of the great difficulties about the old *chin* repertoire is that methods of notation and scoring have changed with each succeeding century. Although there is a collection of music dating back over twenty centuries, no present-day players can read these scores and only a few musicians are able to read those that are two and three hundred years old. Since 1954 some extensive research has been carried out on many of the old scores, and the experts have been able to transliterate several into legible playing form. One of the most recent achievements in this field, of which the Chinese are very proud, is the re-scoring of an ancient composition called *Kuanglingsan*, which is thought to be one of the world's earliest recorded musical compositions. The first known references to this work date back about one thousand eight hundred years, and it remained current among musicians until as late as the thirteenth century. The text of the score on which the present research has been done dates from the Ming dynasty, when it was published in a collection known as *The Mysterious Score*.

The research was carried out by Kuan Ping-hu, a musician and a *chin* specialist of some fifty years standing, who had previously done some study on the ancient score. He spent two years on his task which was a complex one since ancient notations written in Chinese have no marking bars, length of note or rhythm, and the complicated symbols used as directions for playing are often abbreviated. Kuan finished his task in 1955, when *Kuanglingsan* in his contemporary rendering was published and performed (see Plate 15).

Obviously one man's interpretation of a work like this is always open to differences of opinion by other musicologists, but the intention and achievement behind research of this nature commands respect. There is less cause for admiration in announcements that old compositions have been "adapted" for improved types of *chin* which have been made with a larger sound volume and are being used for concert work. There is a suspicion of bastardisation here that prevails too frequently in Marxist experiments in the fields of art. *Chin* have always been made by skilled craftsmen and handed on from generation to generation, rather in the way that a Stradivari violin is cherished in the West. Today there is a Chinese Musical Instruments Factory in Soochow that is reported to be manufacturing *chin* by the hundreds and four "improved" types are said to have been introduced. The old Ming masters must surely turn in their graves.

A second ancient musical instrument that has returned to new popularity is the *p'i-p'a*, which came to China via Central Asia and was used in the court orchestras of the T'ang dynasty (618–906 A.D.). Within more recent times it has been used by the sing-song girls, as the samisen is used by the Japanese geisha, and also as an instrument to provide accompaniment for certain types of story-tellers, particularly those in the Soochow area. There are no sing-song girls today, but the story-tellers are still extremely active as we have seen in the chapter on theatre.

The *p'i-p'a* is also a solo instrument for more serious-minded Chinese musicians and is used in playing narrative pieces requiring dazzling displays of fingering. A typical example is the piece called *Ambuscade of Ten Sides*, said to have been composed in the Sui dynasty (589–618 A.D.), and musically descriptive of a famous battle in history. The composition is divided into twenty short movements with titles like "The Armies Assembled," "Dividing into Regiments," "Drum Beats," "Signals," "Firing Guns," "Bugles," "City Gates Breached," and so on, down to the final movement depicting the suicide of the defeated commander. The enthusiasts never tire of pieces like this or the virtuosity required to play them. Another well-known *p'i-p'a* solo, composed in the T'ang dynasty, is called *Moon Rising High*, and is a tone poem describing the full moon as seen in twelve different landscape settings.

Radio and records have done a great deal to restore the popularity of instruments like the *chin* and the *p'i-p'a*. The latter has always been used in theatre orchestras, but historical films have given both instruments an extra function. Long-playing records are being made of all famous pieces like *Kuanglingsan* and *Ambuscade of Ten Sides*. The record industry in China has been greatly expanded for the coverage of traditional music, and some very useful discs are being produced from the point of view of historical recording. Before 1949 the bulk of Chinese recordings were either "yellow music" or excerpts from famous traditional dramas and story-telling repertoires, all on 78 shellac discs. Within recent years long-playing records have been produced in increasing quantities in the three standard rpm sizes. There is now a more extensive coverage of traditional drama, ballad singing, instrumental playing, and folk song than has ever existed before. The Ministry of Culture has sponsored a programme for recording performances of famous old artists in the various areas. One example is a complete series of Sinkiang ballads that were put into discs as the result of searching out the few performers of them still left. Production of records is still not enough to meet demands, and their quality is not as high as their Western equivalents, nevertheless standards are good and the various musical and dramatic arts of China are being preserved in permanent form on a scale impossible before.

Musical activities in contemporary China can be described as flourishing, in spite of the dismal restraints imposed by Party cultural directives. Certainly in the field of traditional music, there has been research and recording of lasting value. The good outweighs the bad, of which there is also full measure, but, as suggested earlier, time is inexorably on the side of good art.

In the field of Western-style music, the body of trained instrumentalists and vocalists is growing, and public appreciation being widened by concerts and broadcasts. The new performers are young, lack experience, and are burdened by political restraints, but technically they progress and that is something. That China has nothing distinguished to show in the way of new creative music is due to both a lack of seasoned composers and the hindering hand of the Party, but there is possibly a deeper problem beneath these obvious facts. Nearly forty years ago the Russian composer, Alexandre Tcherepnin, visited China and was concerned about Chinese attitudes towards music in general, the Western influences they admired, and their indifference to their own background. He suggested that the Chinese should study a harmony employing the pentatonic scale with modulations, and to emphasise his points he worked out a piano study course on the pentatonic scale for the use of the Shanghai Conservatory students. In his lectures he declared that the Chinese could learn nothing from Handel or Beethoven, and that if they succumbed to Western music they should study impressionistic composers like Debussy and Stravinsky. Tcherepnin had a point; undoubtedly China could benefit by some rethinking along these lines if she is to develop a creative tradition in the Western idiom. But so long as Chinese composers are expected to be auditory illustrators of political clichés it remains difficult, for this has nothing to do with music or art.

VIII. THE CHINESE OUTSIDE CHINA

Economic and political factors have driven large communities of Chinese overseas in the past, and the process has been repeated on a new scale since the advent of Communism. Until the Sino-Japanese War the resident Chinese populations spread throughout Southeast Asia and the United States were mainly the descendants of artisans and traders. Their very prosperous communities were commercial in both purpose and outlook. They retained a pattern of traditional culture, but only in a conservative way. Most activities in theatre, painting, or writing (chiefly journalism) that went on in these communities were far behind developments on the mainland in any contemporary sense.

The war changed this in several ways. There were shifts in population, which meant that post-war colonial Chinese communities were infiltrated by a more intellectual class from the mainland. This was noticeable in a colony like Hong Kong where, to take a practical example, the Chinese press developed much higher general literary standards than before.

The war also ended many sharp social divisions and prejudices that had previously existed between Chinese and Western communities, and there was a greater communication. Increased rapport between East and West brought a better level of appreciation of each other's cultural standards.

But the most violent changes came when the Communists conquered the mainland in 1949 and the Nationalists retreated to Taiwan to set up a government that, they declared, was the legitimate one of China. In addition, the Chinese population of Hong Kong was swollen several times beyond its normal size by the constant flow of refugees from the North. These included university professors, teachers, artists, film stars, and others, all of whom had subsequent effects on the cultural situation in Hong Kong, until then dominated by a predominately commercial Cantonese community.

Hong Kong in its turn became a centre for emigration to the United States, which offered increased hospitality to the Chinese. New York today, for example, has a Chinese population of approximately 50,000, about half of whom have come since 1949. It is one of the largest Chinese groups in relation to area outside of Southeast Asia, and obviously it is going to grow.

A decade has now passed, and the majority of the Chinese immigrants have become successfully assimilated within American society, for the Chinese are the most adaptable and most peaceful people of any who leave their homelands to settle abroad. What future effect their domicile is going to have on the cultural background of the new Chinese population, and particularly, their children, remains to be seen. Language is the great problem. A second generation has to forget its own tongue, and with that goes literature. Obviously there can be no hope of the United States nourishing a new school of Chinese writers. A Chinese who writes in English can make little contribution to his own literature.

The problem becomes less rigid in other artistic fields which are not bound in quite the same way as literature. There are one or two Chinese artists at work in the United States who suggest a new horizon beyond the present political extremism of Communist China and the escapism of Taiwan. But before going on to discuss their work in detail it will be useful to consider first the position of the arts generally in Taiwan and Hong Kong. They are the two major areas of Chinese population adjoining the mainland, through which the Chinese population in America has come.

TAIWAN

The cream of the literary and artistic world declined to follow the Nationalist Government into exile in 1949, preferring to face events on the mainland. From the beginning, therefore, Taiwan has suffered under a grave disadvantage in being deprived of a majority of the best creative minds in the arts. In addition, the Nationalist Government has pursued an ostrich-like policy towards cultural developments on the mainland, ignoring the fact that so many of the reforms and innovations in artistic matters there have evolved from causes they themselves espoused in the old days. Moreover, a fanatical censorship bans the work of some of the best writers of the post-May Fourth period, so that the younger generation in Taiwan are deprived of a major part of modern Chinese literature. This has resulted in a spiritual claustrophobia that is inimical to any creative surge among contemporary writers and artists. Cut off from the main stream of their own tradition and sandwiched between the political antagonisms of China and America, the best that a new generation can hope to achieve is a form of escapism.

And as one American historian has said: "The Nationalist regime has not in fact provided an effective rallying point for intellectuals and youth among the large number of anti-communists but non-Kuomintang Chinese who are scattered all over the world, in Hong Kong and elsewhere. Recently, it is true, a few prominent intellectuals, such as the scholar and former diplomat Hu Shih, have been attracted back to Taiwan [where he died in 1962], but the Nationalists have retained a deep apprehension about subversion. . . ."*

* A. Doak Barnett, *Communist China and Asia,* p. 395.

The last clause can be considered a charitable under-statement in view of certain occurrences relating to journalism in Taiwan. In March 1960, the Grand Assembly of the International Press Institute meeting in Tokyo was compelled to decide that the standards of press freedom in Taiwan did not justify their approving Nationalist newspaper editors for membership on the Institute's executive board. Nor did a series of events in October 1960 show any reason for negating the decision. In that month Lei Chen, the editor of the *Free China Fortnightly,* was arrested, given a military trial, and sentenced to ten years' imprisonment plus a seven-year deprivation of citizen's rights. The unfortunate editor's crime was in allowing fearless criticism of government abuses and power in the columns of his magazine, which one Chinese literary man called "a leading journal of opinion." For this the Nationalists trumped up a charge of sedition and passed a savage sentence that made nonsense of every circumstance in which the adjective "free" is so liberally used by them. In such a climate the creative writer has a thin time. His profession is a thankless one from any point of view in Taiwan.

A one-time Taipei editor, Hsia Tsi-au, has said, in reference to the city's literary coteries, that if the writers have not produced any outstanding works they can at least be proud of taking no orders from others regarding their literary integrity. He qualified this by adding that because all Taiwan writers had to earn their living by anything but writing, they tended to be extraverts who enjoyed a social-club existence rather than trying to be dedicated hermits.

A great deal of the younger writers' work is done for various magazines and newspapers and tends to be proportionately light in character. The short story is a very popular medium, and there is also a considerable quantity of poetry being written. Among the writers are some with established reputation and considerable circulation by Taiwan standards. One such is Meng Yao (Yang Tsung-chen, 1919–   ), a woman author who has several novels to her name and is an associate professor at Taiwan Normal University. A second is Wang Lan (1922–   ), a member of the National Assembly and the author of several books, one of which, a novel called *Blue and Black*, has gone into several editions. (An edition averages about two thousand copies in Chinese publishing.)

The poets, as poets do, have organised themselves in various "schools," the oldest of which is the Blue Star Group founded in 1954. The work of its members is to be found in different magazines and newspapers, and several collections of verse have been published. Every style of Western poetry is emulated, while a second group, the Modernists, founded in 1955, have as their avowed aim to take present-day Chinese poetry beyond the finest limits of the contemporary Western verse idioms.

Set apart from these younger writers with their heterogeneous modes and air of fatalistic resignation to their environment, there are some old-timers of the Chinese literary scene who deserve detailed mention here. One is Liang Shih-ch'iu, born in Peking in 1902, a literary critic and translator of Shakespeare. He was a member of the New Moon Group and a contemporary of the poets Hsü Chih-mo and Wen I-to.

Liang was educated in Peking and in 1923 went to the United States where he entered Colorado College and was a fellow student of Wen I-to. After taking his degree he moved on to Harvard University and then to Columbia and returned to Peking in 1926. From there he went to Shanghai and took up university teaching. Shanghai in the thirties was a lively centre of literary debates and furious argument. The protagonists of writing as a political weapon were very much to the fore. Liang, as a member of the New Moon Group, regarded the leftist viewpoint with scorn. The idea of proletarian literature was anathema to his soul. He fought every inch of the way for the artistic rights of the individual and literary expression unsullied by any dogma that opposed freedom of creative effort. He was a redoubtable spokesman for his case and gained considerable public notice, the more so since the stand he took brought him into sharp argument with the celebrated Lu Hsün, the leader of the opposition and himself no mean advocate.

Eventually Liang retired from the heat of literary battle to become head of the English literature department at National Peking University, but he published several volumes of critical essays re-stating his principles and literary faith. During his period at Peking University, where he went in 1934, Liang published a number of translations of Shakespeare's plays, including *Hamlet, Macbeth, As You Like It, Othello,* and *A Midsummer Night's Dream.* Shakespearian study has absorbed him for most of his career, and the translations have been a labour of love.

Liang left Peking for Chungking in 1937 and was employed in the National Bureau of Translation and Compilation during the war. He returned to Peking as professor of English literature at the Normal College after the war and went to Taiwan in 1949 to become head of the English language department of the Taiwan Normal University. He is now living in retirement in Taipei, a veteran of a literary era on whose rolls his name is written large.

Two other Taiwan literary old-timers are women, Hsieh Ping-ying (1908–), who writes under the pen name Ping-ying, and Su Hsüeh-lin (1897–). They are personalities of contrasting types. Ping-ying was a militant revolutionary who made her literary reputation with a novel recording her experiences as a woman auxiliary at the battle front during the early days of the Nationalists' struggle for control of China. Su Hsüeh-lin, on the other hand, is an academic writer, a poet, and an authority on ancient verse forms, as well as an essayist and short-story writer.

Ping-ying was born in Hunan, celebrated in China as

the home of revolutionaries, including Mao Tse-tung. She was very independent as a child and refused to conform to the traditional custom of foot-binding. Given her early education by her father, a classical scholar, Ping-ying later defied her mother's wishes by insisting on attending a modern girls' school run by missionaries. She was finally expelled from this institution for leading a student demonstration against the Japanese but later continued her education at another school where she developed interests in literature, both Chinese and Western. After graduation in 1926 she entered the Central Military and Political Academy where she was subjected to a rigorous training and sent out to join the Revolutionary army as a member of a specially recruited girls' corps. While on active service in the war that established the Nationalist regime, she wrote her *War Diary*, which was published serially in the *Central Daily News* and simultaneously translated into English by Lin Yü-t'ang. Translated into several other languages later, the book brought Ping-ying world-wide literary notice. Women fighters have always been favourite characters in old Chinese fiction and on the stage, but this was the first occasion for a modern public to be able to meet one in the flesh and read her diary in the bargain.

In spite of this unorthodox career, Ping-ying returned home after the war to be forced into an arranged marriage by her parents. But she deserted her bridegroom immediately after the wedding and fled to Shanghai. Further study, teaching, and writing followed her break with domestic bondage, and when the Japanese attacked Shanghai in 1932 she returned to active military service once more. In 1935 she went to Japan but was arrested in the following year and thrown into prison for six weeks as a political suspect. In 1936 she published her *Autobiography of a Woman Soldier* which was translated into English and widely read and discussed. During the first years of the war Ping-ying organised a women's corps and did some front-line reporting before taking up an academic career in Ch'engtu. After the war she taught in Peking and left for Taiwan when the Communists came. Here she continues with her teaching and writing, a link with days when women's independence took on a new meaning in China.

Su Hsüeh-lin, the second of our women writers, came from Anhwei and, after graduating from college in Peking in 1921, went to study in Lyon, France, until 1925. On her return to China she took up an academic career and taught at various schools and universities. In 1928 she published her *Green Sky*, a collection of stories and prose, and, in 1929, her autobiographical novel, *Mourning Heart*, which made her literary reputation. It was one of the most popular books among girl students during the thirties, and it has run through ten editions. The novel embodied some of her own experiences in France and the emotional stress she suffered through various family troubles and her conversion to Catholicism in 1924. She embodied her own philosophy in the book, which dwelt on the complexities of life's problems. Briefly, her faith was that the love of a mother for her child, or between man and woman, provided the greatest balm to life's wounds. But Su Hsüeh-lin was a patriot as well as a romantic. She had a deep consciousness of her country's suffering and a staunch belief in the rights of the individual. The mind of a progressive woman in the revolutionary era was epitomised in her characters.

During her long academic career Su Hsüeh-lin has made an intensive study of mythology and the poetry of the Ch'u era (740–330 B.C.). Her researches in these fields have enabled her to advance some original theories on the cultural relations between the East and West during an early period of man's history. Su Hsüeh-lin is an admirer of France and French hospitality and made her second visit to Paris in 1950–52 to do some literary research. Today she is teaching and is connected with the Ministry of Education in Taiwan.

One of Taiwan's most distinguished literary elders is, or rather was, for he has died as this chapter is being written, Ch'i Ju-shan. Ch'i Ju-shan came from Hopei and belonged to an old scholar family. He himself received a classical education in the old style and took his degree under the traditional examination system. Afterwards he studied French and German at a school of foreign languages run by the government in Peking. In 1908 he began travelling regularly to France as an escort to Chinese students going to Paris, and while on these trips he saw a great deal of Western theatre and opera. The experience stimulated him to work for a renaissance in China's traditional theatre. In 1913 he became acquainted with the actor, Mei Lan-fang, then a rising young star in Peking. Ch'i made some suggestions for improving stage technique in one of Mei's plays. This led to a greenroom connection between the two men that eventually ripened into an artistic partnership of some twenty years' standing. In 1915 Ch'i wrote and devised a new play for Mei based on a famous old legend and called *Ch'ang O Flies to the Moon*. It was the first of a long series, more than twenty in all, Ch'i wrote for Mei which incorporated new dances based on old choreography as well as costumes designed in authentic period styles.

Ch'i made a thorough and intensive study of the traditional theatre, watching performances, interviewing actors and musicians, reading scripts, and all the time making copious notes which were later embodied in a series of books he wrote on various technical aspects of the traditional Peking drama. There was no point of theatre lore in which he was not versed and which he had not tracked down to a source. Ch'i was a veritable encyclopaedia of theatre knowledge. When the writer met him in Taiwan in 1957 Ch'i used the leisurely intervals between the courses at a Chinese banquet to discourse on the conventionalised cough used in some roles on the stage. The pity is that over the years it was not possible to make recordings of Ch'i talking on the theatre. Much has died with him, for although he has left a wealth of material in his writings, it was in spontaneous conversation that the extent of his knowledge was revealed in its most fascinating aspect.

Ch'i was responsible for many of the arrangements for Mei Lan-fang's tour in the United States in 1930; in fact, it could truthfully have been called his brain child, for it was something he worked for all through his association with Mei, whom he accompanied to the United States. Among other things he prepared the illustrative material that was used for the enlightenment of the Western audiences.

Ch'i's association with Mei Lan-fang ended in 1931 when Japanese hostilities in Manchuria caused the actor to move his headquarters to Shanghai. During the war Ch'i remained in Peking, living more or less as a recluse and safeguarding a small drama museum which was his especial care. He left for Taiwan in 1948 and remained there until his death. In many ways his exile was a lonely one, for the great stage personalities, with whom he passed so much of his working life, stayed on the mainland. Ch'i's death followed that of Mei by less than a year, the finale to a great theatre partnership that had been severed by the vagaries of war and revolution.

The Theatre, Dance, and Film in Taiwan

It is appropriate to pass from Ch'i Ju-shan to a brief survey of theatre, brief in a double sense, for Taiwan can never hope to compete with the wealth and diversity of theatrical activity on the mainland. From 1949 until her marriage in 1955, Ku Cheng-ch'iu, a student of Mei Lan-fang, ran her own troupe in Taipei, and it was very popular. Afterwards, the theatrical pride of Taiwan was the Ta P'eng, or the Great Roc Troupe, recruited from personnel of the air force, an example that has caused other armed-service branches to form their own troupes. When this writer saw the Great Roc Troupe in 1957 they were technically far inferior to any equivalent troupe on the mainland, although since then they have had time to mature a little. The Great Roc Troupe visited Europe in 1957, but it was to their detriment that a troupe from Peking had been there two years before and dazzled London and Paris with their skill and precision. A well-known London ballet critic, Alexander Bland, wrote of the Great Roc Troupe: "Our innocence is gone. Never again after the visit of the company from Peking two years ago can we experience the full *frisson* of meeting for the first time the strange beauty of the Chinese classical theatre face to face. . . . It would be rash for a Westerner to make a snap judgement. But the finish, timing, and style do not seem the equal of the Peking company. . . ."

Since 1957 Taiwan has developed three "schools" for training children in traditional theatrical art. Of these the Fuhsing School of Dramatic Arts, a private academy founded by Wang Chen-tsu, has become the best known and embodies a curriculum in the old style with general education included. There are said to be some promising students among the boys and girls belonging to this school. The two other training groups for children are a junior version of the Great Roc Troupe and a group belonging to the National School of Arts. In spite of these late attempts to revive a sound traditional theatre in Taiwan the results are but a pale reflection of what goes on in China proper.

In dance too there has been a concerted attempt to follow mainland precedents. In 1952 a National Dance Promotion Committee was formed and May 5 set aside for an annual dance festival. On this date competitions are held for performances in various traditional and minority group dances. The Taiwan dance movement is probably strongest in schools and educational institutions where performances attain a good level of accomplishment. But it is necessary only to see the vulgarised, tourist promotion of the aboriginal dancers at the celebrated Sun Moon

Lake resort to realise what a long way the Taiwan authorities are yet from any true conception of folk-dance preservation.

The Taiwan film industry is on a comparatively small scale, and its standards of production have much in common with Hong Kong studios, with whom there is a good deal of interchange of "stars." The principal Taiwan studio is the Central Motion Picture Corporation of Free China where the majority of the feature films are made. A certain amount of documentary production goes on, such as *Agriculture in Taiwan,* which won a special award at the 1956 Asian Film Festival and is an example of several pictures made by the Taiwan Film Studio. Taiwan films in general carry on the old Shanghai tradition and, like the Hong Kong productions, seem unable to rise beyond trite and hackneyed themes. Nothing produced in Taiwan is within comparable range of the better films of Japan and India.

Taiwan's entry for the 1960 Asian Film Festival was a good example of the level of production. Entitled *Paternal Love,* it was produced by the Central Motion Picture Corporation. The story is about a man released from prison after a twenty-year sentence for manslaughter who starts life again as a driver. The inevitable happens, and he meets his former wife whose father has forced her to remarry in spite of her having a son by her ex-convict husband. He is taken to meet the son, who is not informed of his father's identity. However, the son's rival in love discovers it and spreads the news. The son's girl jilts him as a result, and the unhappy boy runs away to plunge into a life of gambling. Moved by paternal love, the ex-convict father seeks out his errant son and, in rescuing him from the toils of gamblers, kills a gangster. Everyone is moved by his devotion to his son as he gives himself up to the police.

The role of the mother in this film was played by Lu Pi-yün, a veteran actress who started her career as a "straight" actress in Shanghai and has recently returned to the Taiwan screen after a two-year absence. She made her film reputation in a film entitled *Flight,* in which she took the part of a young student victimised by the Communists, a role which, according to a Chinese columnist, "drew the tears of many movie goers."

In addition to commercial production, there is a certain amount of educational film making in Taiwan. The Chung Hua Educational Films Workshop was established in 1955 in Taipei, and eight films were produced in the first eighteen months of activity. They included titles like *Chinese Ceramics* and *The Third National Boy Scout Jamboree.*

In closing this survey of Taiwan, some mention must be made of the fine arts and music. The National Academy of Arts and Crafts, founded in 1955, and the National Taiwan Art Hall, founded in 1957, are most active in these. The National Academy offers five-year courses in traditional drama, modern drama, and music. The traditional theatre school was formerly under the nominal direction of Ch'i Ju-shan. The modern drama department is directed by Li Man-kuei, a woman university professor who graduated from Yenching and Columbia Universities and is herself a playwright. Music is under the charge of Shen Hsüeh-yung, a well-known singer. She was born in Szechuan and made her professional debut from the Provincial College of Arts there. A soprano, she studied opera singing at the Liceo Musicale Isabella Rosati in Rome during the early fifties, and while in Italy gave several recitals. She has since sung in Japan, Thailand, and the Philippines and has made many appearances on international television and radio. In 1960 she was officially invited by the State Department to study musical education in America, where she gave several concerts. Musical research in Taiwan goes on at the National Research Institute of Music, established in 1957 under the direction of Cesar C. K. Teng, a violinist, which sponsors concerts from time to time.

Exhibitions of painting are held in the National Taiwan Art Hall, which also serves as a theatre and concert hall. National art exhibitions are held periodically in the Taiwan Provincial Museum and consist of representative displays of both Chinese and Western-style painting. One of the more popular artists in Taiwan is Ran In-ting (1902–   ), born in Taiwan of Chinese parentage. He studied in Japan from 1920–23, and the Japanese influence is apparent in much of his work. An academic watercolourist whose paintings combine the virtuosity of the medium with a certain slickness of handling, he has exhibited abroad in both the United States and Europe. His monochrome sketches are closest to the traditional Chinese style, although the figures in many of his brush drawings and the compositional arrangements of his landscape betray the strong influence of Western academism. His figure sketches show a lively sense of movement and character, but they are not very deep. Ran In-ting is an illustrator rather than a creative painter.

Again, as in dance, Taiwan's best artistic activities go on at the educational level, although here it is often difficult for the objective observer not to feel that what the mainland does today, Taiwan tries to do tomorrow.

HONG KONG

The educated Chinese population of Hong Kong before the war was largely drawn from the compradore-merchant class. Most of them had their ancestral roots in the neighbouring mainland province of Kwangtung, and, generally speaking, they were a very provincially minded community. They used their Cantonese dialect in both their schools and their businesses, although as a matter of commercial necessity a good proportion of them spoke English as a second language. Interest in the arts, where it existed at all, was conservative and not particularly high in standards of taste. There were some exceptions among

the business community, a few of whom had a knowledgeable interest in traditional Chinese theatre and music. A
group of such men clubbed together in 1922 and invited
Mei Lan-fang to perform in Hong Kong. It was a historic
event in local Chinese circles and unique of its kind. But
the wealthier Chinese preferred to donate their money to
causes that put them in good standing with the colonial
government rather than set themselves up as patrons of
the arts.

If the Hong Kong Chinese were indifferent to the arts,
the colonial British on their side had little to offer. Pre-war
Hong Kong for all its resources and wealth was culturally
starved. There was no theatre, music, or painting, except
on the most amateur basis. There was not even a public
library. The old City Hall opened in 1869, the one good
theatre-concert hall the colony ever possessed, was pulled
down in a dilapidated condition in 1935 to make room for
extensions to the leading bank, and nothing was put up to
replace it until 1962. Altogether there was not a very
propitious atmosphere for the meeting of Eastern and
Western cultures.

It would, however, be invidious in any discussion of
Chinese cultural activities in pre-war Hong Kong to omit
mention of the name of Hsü Ti-shan, a notable literary
figure in his own right and a man who did a great deal
to advance the cause of Chinese arts and letters in the
philistine colony. Hsü Ti-shan (1893–1941) was not a
Cantonese. He was born in Taiwan of a Fukien family
and educated in Peking. In addition he studied at both
Columbia and Oxford Universities.

Hsü was one of the founder members of the Society for
Literary Research, discussed earlier in this book, and he
made a considerable reputation as a writer of short stories. His first collection was published in 1925 under the
title *The Vain Labours of a Spider*. His intellectual interests were wide; he became known as a specialist in the
comparative study of Oriental religions and Christianity,

and he also carried out some extensive anthropological researches.

In 1936 Hsü was invited to leave his post at Yenching University in Peking to become the first professor of Chinese at the University of Hong Kong. Hu Shih had declined the post but recommended Hsü. Hsü was at first reluctant to leave China for a colonial university that in those days had not too high a reputation in Chinese academic circles, and which was run like a British university, designed to turn out Chinese students in the British mould. Paradoxically enough, the institution had been built entirely with the money of a Parsee merchant who had made his fortune on the old opium exchange of the eighteen-seventies. Without his benevolence it is questionable whether Hong Kong would ever have had a university. Its chief pride was a good medical school which technically claimed Dr. Sun Yat-sen as a graduate. Sun, in fact, was a licentiate of the old Hong Kong Medical College, a private institution founded in 1887 from which he graduated many years before the university was founded. When Parsee generosity made a British university possible, the Hong Kong Medical College, already in process of taking over a new site, agreed to be amalgamated as a faculty and in doing so bestowed the Sun Yat-sen legend on its new parent body.

The university spent the first twenty years of its existence in constant debt. It was nobody's child. The colonial government's attitude towards supporting anything so unproductive of revenue as a university was lukewarm. Among the Chinese there was resentment at the autocratic attitude of the university authorities in keeping the highest academic appointments as a closed preserve, even when able and well qualified Chinese were available. It was characteristic of the system that, although it opened in 1911, the university never got around to appointing a professor of Chinese until 1936.

Hsü Ti-shan therefore accepted the new appointment

with some trepidation. But because the university had at last bowed to the strong feelings of Chinese academic circles, Hsü was persuaded to become a pioneer for the sake of his people. It turned out to be a very successful choice from all points of view. Hsü formed a rallying point for students, who felt that at last they had a worthy intellectual representative of their own, and he did a good deal to advance knowledge of the Chinese background in the Western community. Among the lectures in English that he gave, for example, was a series on the history of Chinese costume.

Hsü Ti-shan's sudden and early death was a great loss to the Chinese community in Hong Kong. He established a precedent and symbolised the beginning of a breakdown in prejudice and apathy between the two societies. And he inspired many of the younger Chinese with a new respect for their culture, which they tend either to forget or despise in the Westernisation due to their environment.

A sad factor in the continued proximity of the Hong Kong Chinese to more superficial Western cultural influences was the debasement of their own traditional arts. The most glaring example was in the theatre. The Cantonese theatre in Hong Kong was originally a direct off-shoot of the great mainland tradition with its highly developed formalism. The same plays were performed, and the same qualities of acting were savoured, by the connoisseurs in Hong Kong as in China proper. The great difference was the use of the Cantonese dialect, which meant differences in the style of singing and rhythmic emphasis. Although Hong Kong never had a large theatre quarter, and in the years after 1911 many young people were no longer interested, the old drama always had a following among the older generation.

But by the early nineteen-thirties the Cantonese theatre in Hong Kong had become a debased form and has remained so into present times. The idol of the pre-war Hong Kong theatre was Ma Si-tsang, a talented and versatile actor, skilled in the old style of acting and an educated man who had started life as a schoolmaster. He retained his position after the war, and until 1955, Ma, and his wife and ex-pupil, Hung Sin-nui, a popular stage and screen actress, were the top ranking pair in the Hong Kong theatre world.

Strangely enough, during the thirties it was Ma Si-tsang and others like him who took to re-hashing Western material for stage productions. For instance, he staged shows based on the films *The Thief of Bagdad* and *The Love Parade*. His stage wardrobe included everything from the outfit of a Spanish grandee to a Western dinner jacket. The popular film and the second-rate musical instead of the legends and sagas of the past were his inspiration, and concoctions of the most dubious origin were served up to meet the debased tastes of the Hong Kong theatre-going public. To make matters worse, the cornet, the saxophone, and the violin had become part of the traditional theatre orchestra.

Actors like Ma Si-tsang have always complained that they were forced into this kind of thing to keep alive; that it was the only method by which they could gain support from the commercially minded managements of Hong Kong. The result has been that the true Cantonese theatre is dead in Hong Kong today. The contemporary version has become a species of Chinese "musical" in which the saxophone is the principal instrument to which all the musical forms are accommodated. Costumes are vulgarised, and the gestures and postures of the old stage, sloppily rendered, if they are attempted at all. Realistic stage sets are reminiscent of the worst type of small-town Christmas pantomime. The Cantonese theatre of Hong Kong is despised by most educated Chinese, and with some reason.

The old-time Hong Kong theatre-goers have nevertheless been provided with food for thought in recent years by the programme of reform in the Cantonese theatre on the mainland. There dignity has been restored to this provincial form once again. In 1955 Ma Si-tsang and Hung Sin-nui returned to the mainland amid a flood of rumours about their personal affairs. Since that time they have been set to work as a team carrying out a programme of reform in the Cantonese drama, and a number of very successful films as well as plays have resulted from this partnership. Some of the films have been shown in Hong Kong and played to packed houses. One of the most recent was based on a story by Kuan Han-ch'ing (1280–1368), a famous old dramatist. There is a vast gulf between these new productions, on both stage and screen, and the kind of trite material that occupied this talented husband-wife team in the old days.

There is one Hong Kong amateur, Kwok On, a banker, who has devoted a lifetime of study to the old Chinese drama and particularly the puppet theatre. He owns what is probably the finest collection of old Cantonese puppets in existence and himself runs a puppet theatre. To help him in his researches he has rounded up the last few old puppeteers in Hong Kong, where they gave performances to the public during the 1960 Arts Festival. Over the years Kwok has also been taking extensive notes on old theatre techniques from an aged Cantonese actor who is the last of his kind in Hong Kong. In his quiet way Kwok has done a service to the Chinese puppet theatre that is every bit as valuable as some of the more spectacular events one hears about on the mainland.

The Hong Kong Chinese film industry, to which reference has been made earlier, expanded rapidly in the post-war years. There are now eight major studios and a number of smaller companies who rent studio space as and when required. The films are made largely with an eye on Chinese communities elsewhere—there is a great demand from overseas Chinese audiences for films in the Cantonese dialect which is widely spoken throughout the Southeast Asian communities—and their production is looked upon as a business operation first and foremost; profitable returns must be guaranteed. As a result production costs are kept at a minimum while quantity precedes quality.

The star system is the curse of the Hong Kong film world where all the paraphernalia of Hollywood-style publicity is used to glamourise young men and women who, truth to tell, often have very little beyond their looks. "Stars" come and go with surprising rapidity; trim figures and pretty faces are far easier to find than genuine acting talent in Hong Kong.

The Hong Kong film producer is unhampered by the ideological control suffered by his mainland equivalent, but he has his own restriction in the damning business of "giving the public what it wants." Social-political differences are not always so sharply resolved in terms of right and left among the Chinese as the propagandists would have us believe. The screen provides a surprisingly common denominator for the human message. This is what the Hong Kong film makers have still to learn, or have forgotten.

Post-war Hong Kong is nonetheless a changed place generally from pre-war days. Complacency towards the arts is by no means dead and the spirit of amateurism still reigns, but music, theatre, and painting are now recognised as important in education, and at the educational level great progress has been made.

Western musical education has increased by leaps and bounds among the Hong Kong Chinese. Close on two thousand candidates sit for the local examinations of the Associated Boards of the Royal Schools of Music in London every year, and among several talented young people now being trained there are signs of one or two distinguished talents-to-be. But there is often a sharp gap between these children's Western training and a knowledge of their own cultural background, which few of them understand very deeply and many not at all. And today there is an increasing proportion of Chinese teen-agers in Hong Kong for whom "pop" singers represent the peak of Western, and Eastern, musical achievement.

In the dramatic field, youthful activity has been stimulated by an inter-schools drama competition which is held every year. Usually the plays are specially written or adapted and cover both Chinese historical and contemporary themes. The Chinese have a natural feeling for acting—it is only necessary to watch two Shanghai businessmen discussing a deal to realise this—and there are some quite talented youngsters on the school stage in Hong Kong. Their greatest fault is one that afflicts the modern Chinese theatre at a more professional level also —indifferent elocution and a passion for drawing out trivial action at the expense of dramatic tension.

On a more adult basis, there are a number of amateur Chinese painting and dramatic clubs. Since 1954 Hong Kong has held an annual Arts Festival at which local talent is displayed in performances and exhibitions held for the public's benefit. Hong Kong has arrived at a maturer conception of the arts rather late in the century, and while this festival of local achievements is excellent in itself, it tends to become repetitive without any first-class talent from outside against which to measure its worth.

Hong Kong is still starved of concerts, exhibitions, and dramatic performances by top-ranking professional artists and performers from the Western world. On the Chinese side, there have been several traditional theatre-dance troupes who have visited Hong Kong from the mainland within recent years and have attracted local audiences with their dramatic skill. The packed and enthusiastic houses to which they have played each time are proof enough that people need little cajoling when the best is there for them to see. Now that Hong Kong has a new City Hall after thirty years without theatre-concert-hall facilities, the prospect seems better for a new era in the arts.

Painting in Hong Kong is served by a number of clubs and societies which sponsor exhibitions of both Western and Chinese forms. Much of the Chinese painting tends to follow well trodden paths, and the old spirit of "amateurism" is very strong. There are many Chinese followers of Western-style painting, most of whom remain faithful to various representational and academic styles with nothing very original to say. The standard of Western-style painting in Hong Kong has for long been at the "sketch club" level, and the Chinese have not had a very deep background of inspiration. Within recent years a small group of both European and Chinese artists has been formed to explore new visual methods. Interesting work has been done by this group, some of whose members have exhibited abroad.

But painting like the other arts suffers from the isolation of Hong Kong. There is no direct connection with any living currents of artistic expression and thought. The Chinese mainland is sealed off, Europe and America are remote. Hong Kong is invariably reduced to falling back on its own resources which by the nature of the situation have become somewhat ingrown.

ENGLAND

Any discussion of Hong Kong must lead back to England whose contacts with China have been largely by way of the Crown Colony. England herself has always had a comparatively small Chinese resident population by United States' standards, but two writers who were working in London before the Second World War demand inclusion in this chronicle. They are Chiang Yee (1903–) and Hsiung Shih-i (1902–). Both men had a considerable reputation in England, the one as a writer-artist and the other as a dramatist.

Chiang Yee began his career as a district magistrate in the first years of the Republic but left China for England during the early thirties to study science. He soon abandoned this to become a lecturer at the London School of Oriental Studies where he first began to write. He developed a fluent and easy English prose style which eventually brought him considerable notice in a series of books written under the pen name of "The Silent Traveller." In these he surveyed his English wanderings in a series of mellow essays illustrated by his own drawings and paintings. *A Chinese Childhood*, published in 1940, was an account of his own upbringing treated in the same way. But his two most significant books were *The Chinese Eye: An Interpretation of Chinese Painting*, published in 1937, and *Chinese Calligraphy*, published the following year. Both books opened up a new world of understanding to ordinary English readers ignorant about the arts of China. Written in an informative but simple style, these two works are classics of their kind. Since the war Chiang has migrated across the Atlantic and is now a faculty member of Columbia University.

Hsiung Shih-i was originally a theatre manager in Peking and Shanghai. He, too, arrived in England in the early thirties, and on the strength of his fluent English and some translations of plays by Sir James Barrie he became familiar with that playwright and his circle. In 1934 Hsiung had his play, *Lady Precious Stream*, accepted by the London producer Leon M. Leon. It took London by storm and Hsiung's fame was made overnight. *Lady Precious Stream* is an English adaptation of incidents from the famous Chinese classical play-cycle *Hung Tsung Lieh Ma* and, as presented on the London stage, was really a kind of whimsical burlesque of Chinese dramatic method. It was not a true Chinese play, in either its faithfulness to the original text or traditional staging. But it was a clever piece of entertainment that endeared itself to Western audiences intrigued by the novelty of the production. It ran for three years and has since passed into the anthologies as the one example of Chinese drama with which the English public was familiar. A film made of *Lady Precious Stream* since the war has not had the success of the original. A new and less susceptible public has grown up since the thirties, perhaps the golden age of Chinese whimsicality in the West. Hsiung wrote several books, but *Lady Precious Stream* remains his best-known work. Today he lives in Hong Kong where he is occupied chiefly with local dramatic activities and journalism.

Until the war, Chiang Yee was the only Chinese painter resident in England, but official cultural relations activities after the war enabled a number of young Chinese artists to study in London. Two of them, Fei Ch'eng-wu and Chang Ch'ing-ying, a woman painter who is now married to Fei, arrived in London in 1946 and stayed on to make their home in England. They have both made a niche for themselves as Royal Academy exhibitors and have also turned their hands to applied arts like textile designing. Fei has further established himself as an illustrator. Both these artists are from Nanking and were former pupils of Hsü Pei-hung.

In the field of music, London now has Peking-born Fu Ts'ung (Fou Ts'ong), a pianist who is a product of Chinese Communist musical education. He also studied in Warsaw where, in 1955, he was a prize winner in the Chopin competition. He afterwards fled to the West and is now permanently settled in London and has married the daughter of Yehudi Menuhin, the violinist. Fu Ts'ung is an accomplished performer with impressive credentials and, to the Chinese, the first pianist of international status they have produced. Fu Ts'ung is perhaps more appreciated in London than New York where he gave his first concert with the New York Philharmonic in 1961. He received only grudging notices. The *New York Times* critic prefaced his unfavourable analysis with the words, "But it cannot be said that his performance on this occasion suggested that the oriental mind can hurdle the cultural barrier," a statement that might have been better put.

THE UNITED STATES

The United States has had especially close ties with China during the last half century. Missionary interests in China have been extensive and closely identified with different aspects of China's Westernisation programme. After first concentrating on the propagation of fundamentalist religion, the missionaries widened the scope of their activities to cover social welfare and the establishment of schools and universities that combined religious instruction with the advantages of a secular education. The nature of her religious-educational role caused America to believe herself essential as a benevolent partner of China, and the involvement took on an emotional significance that has since brought bitter disillusion in its train.

It is not intended to harp on that particular theme here, but rather to discuss the career of a Chinese writer, Lin Yü-t'ang, who, above all others, provided Americans with a literary ideal around which the gossamer of their China dream was woven.

Lin Yü-t'ang (1895–) came from Amoy, and belonged to a Chinese Christian family. His father was a Presbyterian minister, and it was intended that young Lin should follow in his footsteps. He got as far as the theology department of St. John's University in Shanghai when his interest flagged and he renounced Christianity altogether. After a period of teaching English in Peking he left China in 1919 for a period abroad, during which time he took an M.A. at Harvard and a Ph.D. at Leipzig. He returned to Peking in 1923 and took up his academic career again until 1927, when he had a short taste of politics as a secretary in the Foreign Ministry of the new Nationalist Government. Teaching, editing, and philological research occupied his time after that until 1932 when, in Shanghai, he founded a magazine called *The Analect's Fortnightly*.

Lin's purpose was to introduce humour into Chinese

journalism, which he considered far behind its Western counterpart in the lighter forms of social satire. Although he was heavily criticised by both left-wing and extreme right groups for his facetiousness, Lin gathered a talented group of writers around him, and his magazine, which ran until 1935, was a great success. During this period he ran two more magazines: *This Human World,* devoted to developing a popular prose style in journalism, and *The Cosmic Wind,* which modelled itself on the American *Reader's Digest.* Lin also wrote a weekly piece for an English-language journal, *The China Critic,* run by a group of Chinese literary men. Signing himself "The Little Critic," Lin showed himself a clever columnist in the approved Western tradition. In 1935 he joined the editorial staff of the *T'ien Hsia Monthly,* an excellent English-language magazine published by the Sun Yat-sen Institute for Advancement in Culture and Learning. Forced out of publication by the Japanese war, this magazine marked a new peak of sophisticated and cosmopolitan journalism in China.

The end of the *T'ien Hsia Monthly* symbolised the close of Lin Yü-t'ang's career as a brilliant if lightweight journalist with a mastery of English prose style. In 1935 he published his first book, *My Country and My People,* and assumed the role of Chinese sage and philosopher which a romantic and uncritical Western reading public immediately assigned to him. By the time he arrived in New York in 1936 Lin was already a literary lion, and the publication of his second book, *The Importance of Living,* made him an international celebrity whose whimsical interpretations were eagerly accepted for their charm and "old roguery."

Lin's two best-sellers attained an importance in the West that was not borne out in Chinese intellectual circles, where he was regarded as a clever journalist and a good English scholar who knew how to please his Western public. His own people, however, accepted him as neither their interpreter nor a philosopher.

It is necessary only to consider contemporary events in

China when Lin produced his two most popular books to realise the gulf that lay between his urbane essays and a living society. But his witty writing endeared him to a Western public who had always been mentally lazy about China and ever willing to retain the image of oriental charm which Lin knew so well how to conjure up.

Since the success of his first two books, Lin has written a number of novels, the best of which is *Moment in Peking*, published in 1939, a story about contemporary Chinese life that stems from a tradition and has great technical merit. Lin returned to academic life for a brief period in 1954 and became the chancellor of the new Nanyang University in Singapore, but he resigned after six months and returned to the United States. In 1958 Lin publicly announced his re-conversion to the Presbyterian Church; a year later he published his testament entitled *From Pagan to Christian*. The literary "old rogue" was dead, but the image of China that he created had already been buried a decade.

In contrast to the picture of China perpetuated by a writer like Lin Yü-t'ang, there was a less endearing, more sinister image created in the minds of the great cinema-going public in America between the two wars. In the minds of Hollywood producers the word "Chinese" conjured up a recurring vision of tong feuds, opium smokers, gambling dens, slave girls, in fact all the trash from the thriller writer's box of tricks. Even when a film had nothing to do with China a sensational atmosphere was often created by adding a "Chinese" touch. And as someone once commented about one of the more lurid characters of the "Chinatown" school of fiction, "A Chinese wearing Cantonese clothes and named Fu Manchu was about as silly as a Hollander dressed up in Spanish costume and called von McJones." In view of the general attitude about China that existed in Hollywood circles it is not surprising that the first Chinese screen actress in America, Anna May

Wong, was driven to expending her talents on the cinematic travesties of her time.

Anna May Wong (1907–61), was born in Los Angeles
of Cantonese parents. Her father was a laundryman, and
she began her career as a model for a local firm of furriers.
She made her screen debut with a small part in a 1922
film and rose to be one of the great names of Hollywood
during the twenties and thirties. Her first star part was as
the slave girl in the 1924 film *The Thief of Bagdad*, and
her graceful movements, expressive gestures, and thor-
oughly oriental beauty, gained her lasting fame. She became the perfect Hollywood symbol of the "mysterious
East."

In 1929 she went to England and appeared with Lau-
rence Olivier in a stage version of *The Circle of Chalk*
in which her acting was praised by the critics, although
they disapproved of her Los Angeles accent. She made
several films in England after that. The major films, American as well as English, in which she starred during her
career included *Old San Francisco, Shanghai Express,
Limehouse Nights, Chu Chin Chow, Java Head,* and
Daughter of the Dragon. Their titles typify the nature of
the material selected for her.

In 1936 Anna May Wong paid her first visit to China,
genuinely bent on learning the Peking dialect and educating herself in the culture of her people. When asked about
her plans after her period of acclimatisation, she voiced a
desire to refute producers who, when she suggested criticisms, had brusquely answered her, "What do you know
about China, you've never been there?"

The day after her arrival in Hong Kong she was severely criticised by the Chinese press for insulting her race
by her Hollywood interpretations. Somewhat upset by her
bad press, the actress called a special conference at her
hotel and explained to the assembled journalists that she
was not personally responsible for her film roles and that
she was given no say in the matter.

It is possible that, if war had not come, Anna May Wong might have used her considerable acting talents to greater purpose. She was reported at one time to be considering settling in China and carrying on her career there. Instead, events compelled her to return to the old Hollywood routine which held her for the rest of her professional career, and in her later years she showed little reluctance to break away.

THE CONTEMPORARY SCENE

A great deal of water has flowed under the bridge since the era that made Lin Yü-t'ang a prophet and Anna May Wong a star. There can be no more encouraging signs for a new age than the work of the group of people whose descriptions follow. They are two painters, a composer, and an architect. They each have their roots in their own soil, for they were all born in China, but they have all been subjected to Western influences and training in a considerable way. All of them are young and have yet some way to travel on their professional careers, but the body of their accomplishment is impressive enough to warrant their being singled out. Each of them has successfully made the transition in environment, and their art has matured by it. From the crucible of experience they have achieved a harmonious fusion of their creative talents. They form the vanguard of a movement that might become a re-vitalising force in Chinese art of the future.

The two painters, a man and a woman, were born in Peking within a year or two of each other. They are Ch'en Ch'i-k'uan (1921–   ) and Tseng Yu-ho (1923–   ).

Ch'en Ch'i-k'uan studied painting and architecture in his own country before coming to the United States in 1948. He took a degree in architecture at the University of Illinois and then did further study at the University of California. For a period of three years he worked with Walter Gropius and then became a teacher at the Massachusetts Institute of Technology in Cambridge from 1952 to 1954. Subsequently he was associated with I. M. Pei, the architect, discussed later on, and worked on the latter's designs for Tung Hai University in Taiwan. There he was eventually invited to take charge of the architectural department where he is at present, although he intends to return to the United States.

Ch'en has held numerous one-man exhibitions of his painting in New York, Boston, and Chicago. His most recent show at the time of writing, held at the Mi Chou Gallery, New York, during April 1962, revealed him as an artist assured in his talent, sophisticated without having lost his inherent Chinese sense of poetry, and moved by a constant delight in the world around him. In his earlier development Ch'en worked largely in monochrome, but he has now developed an exquisite sense of colouring— restrained, disciplined, and yet with a jewel-like quality that is especially fine in some of his larger compositions. An example is his painting of *The San Marco Cathedral,* an airy tracery of pattern and movement inspired by the flight of pigeons around an ornate spire. The sense of light and atmosphere has a glowing quality that pays homage to Monet.

The influence of Ch'en's architectural training is seen in the precise linear quality of some of his brushwork and in the minute figures and boats that are rendered with an unerring sense of design and movement in many of his landscapes. He has a fondness for aerial perspectives, as in his painting of the great pagoda at Rangoon, and among his favourite themes are junks and fishing-village roofs. His treatment ranges from a closely interwoven mosaic of colour and pattern that fills his long rectangular compositions with delicate flowing rhythms to broad impressionistic renderings whose spatial quality relates him to the great tradition of his artistic ancestry. Ch'en has assimilated his Western idioms understandingly; they never obtrude, nor does he sacrifice his poetic vision for technical effect.

Ch'en's works on Chinese paper with traditional water colours and ink, and his long, narrow rectilinear compositions are reminiscent of the scroll. Of all the Chinese artists working abroad, Ch'en is one who achieves the most perfect balance between the spiritual and technical qualities of the Chinese painter and a modern Western idiom. The great delight of his paintings is in their sense of life and the urgency of his communication. He manages to hold the dream-like moment in time or express sheer delight in the beauties of a landscape. But whatever he has to say is vital and the expression of a sensitive imagination.

Tseng Yu-ho, a woman painter, studied art at Fu Jen University in Peking. She was also a pupil of the Manchu painter Prince P'u Chin, under whom she developed as a skilful exponent of the classical style. In 1945 she married Gustav Ecke, the professor of art history at Fu Jen, and in 1949 they left Peking for Hong Kong where Tseng Yu-ho held an exhibition in the Chinese library of Hong Kong University. The work shown on this occasion marked her as a sensitive artist who handled her medium with an exquisite taste. Her landscapes, rocks, trees, and snow scenes were rendered in the spirit of the great masters of whom she was a worthy follower, but there was as yet no indication of the course her development was to take.

From Hong Kong Tseng Yu-ho settled with her husband in Honolulu, and here her work began to change. The Hawaiian landscape inspired a severer quality in her painting, which, although showing an essentially Chinese treatment in its design and the pictorial rendering of mountains and villages, was clearly moving towards a Western abstractionism. Exhibitions of her new painting in Europe and America brought her notice as one of the more significant modern Chinese painters, and her reputation has grown steadily.

Her most recent exhibition at The Downtown Gallery, New York, in April 1961, showed an interesting new stage in her development. The eighteen large paintings on display incorporated a ninth-century technique used by the old painters to strengthen their scroll paintings—the pasting of thin layers of paper over the silk basis.

After collecting different specimens of paper, both translucent and opaque in their textures, Tseng Yu-ho set about using these to create designs which were reinforced with painting in water colour. Owing to the special nature of the invisible paste, it was possible to paint surfaces of colour beneath overlays of varying thicknesses of paper which revealed the tones at changing depths, causing shimmering rhythms of the most subtle patterns. The abstract harmonies created from these paint-paper formations took as a starting point themes like *The Stream, Song of the Root, Rhapsody in Blue*. The colours were soft, with a feminine delicacy, yet arranged with a powerful grasp of sequence and pattern. In all the paintings the control of space was essentially Chinese in its boldness of design.

Tseng Yu-ho is a very different artist from Ch'en Ch'i-k'uan, who has been less tempted by the fashionable experimenting with new media than his contemporary. But there is nothing superficial about Tseng Yu-ho's meticulous craftsmanship. In lesser hands her style could quickly become mere decoration, but there is a depth in her work that draws the imagination on. Her lyrical sense of creation marks Tseng Yu-ho as an important artist in a direct line with her masters from the past.

From painting we turn to music in the person of the composer Chou Wen-chung, who was born in Shantung in 1923. He came to the United States in 1946 with a scholarship to study architecture at Yale University but abandoned his plans almost immediately and enrolled at the Boston Conservatory of Music where he soon won a scholarship. In 1949 he went to New York where he studied composition and did graduate work at Columbia University. Chou is especially interested in Chinese classical music, on which he has done a great deal of research and whose influence is apparent in his own work, in spirit if not in actual technique.

In 1954 Chou was commissioned by the Louisville Orchestra to compose a triolet for orchestra entitled *And the Fallen Petals*. This was given its first New York performance in 1961 at a Philharmonic concert in Carnegie Hall where it brought the composer a wider public notice. Chou's self-expressed aim in this composition is to convey the emotional qualities of a Chinese landscape painting through the medium of musical sound. He regards himself, in his own words, as "influenced by the philosophy governing every Chinese artist, an affinity to nature in conception, terseness, and allusive expression."

The starting point of his inspiration for this particular composition was in a poem by Meng Hao-jen (689–740 A.D.):

> All through the night
> Such noise of wind and rain
> And the fallen petals
> Who knows how many.

The composition is developed in three parts with a prologue and an epilogue. Chou achieves his tonal "painting" by the use of successions of transparent intervals freely embellished with dissonance in a manner characteristic of Chinese classical music. But Chou also pays homage to Debussy in his work, and in this he would have earned the approval of Tcherepnin, quoted in the chapter on music. Chou uses contemporary Western technique with sensitivity and imagination to achieve his wholly Chinese conception. He has not been heard enough in performance yet for a final estimate of his status as a composer to be given. But his precision, delicacy, and economy of means suggest an assured talent with some interesting achievements ahead of him. A modern Chinese composer is a rare enough bird, and the arrival of one with the imaginative depth of Chou Wen-chung is an omen for a new school of Chinese music.

Last on the list is an architect, Pei Ieoh Ming, who has achieved distinction in his profession at an international level. Pei Ieoh Ming was born in Canton in 1917, although his father was from Shanghai. In 1935 he left China for the United States to study architecture at the Massachusetts Institute of Technology, where he graduated in 1939. During the war he worked for the National Defence Research Committee, and after the war went to Harvard where he took a master's degree in architecture in 1946. He taught at Harvard until 1948. In that year he was chosen architectural designer to William Zeckendorf.

In 1955 he set up his own office in New York and from there executed several commissions in Pittsburgh, Washington, and Chicago. One of his jobs, for which he received an award of merit from the Institute of Architects, was Denver's Mile High Center. This was part of the Zeckendorf Plaza Development in Denver, a well-conceived example of urban re-development for which Pei was the architect and received a First Honor Award of the American Institute of Architects in 1959. In 1961 he received the Arnold W. Brunner Award offered annually by the National Institute of Arts and Letters for excellence in architecture.

One of Pei's most notable recent designs is for the Center for Earth Sciences in his old training school, the Massachusetts Institute of Technology. It is a twenty-story "high rise" building with considerable invention in construction. It has no interior columns, and by omitting them the architect has provided convertible space for library or auditorium purposes. Reinforced concrete piers support the building on either side and also hold mechanical equipment and the elevators. This building exemplifies powers of design and invention that stamp Pei as an architect working in the great traditions of the contemporary masters. It is not too much to claim him as the first Chinese architect to achieve such rank. There is, of course, nothing "Chinese" about Pei's work, unless it be the unerring sense of harmony characteristic of his race. He has absorbed Western contemporary methods but uses them with imagination. The failure to achieve good architecture within China over the last thirty years suggests that it is from men like Pei that the change in heart must come.

On this note it is perhaps fitting to end. Artists in whatever medium learn from each other, whether consciously or otherwise. This is a cardinal principle of growth within any art. And today there is a new internationalism in the arts. An abstract painting done in Tokyo is not recognisably different in technique from one done in New York; the film is the same medium in London or Moscow. It is the more needful then for each country to cherish its own artistic tradition and ensure fertile soil for new growth. China has a superb artistic past from which the West has much to learn. The West in its turn has something to give China. But creative partnership depends on the sincerity of both sides. Chauvinism and political restriction are poisons in the life blood of the arts.

BIBLIOGRAPHY

ENGLISH

The books in the following list are included either for their background information or to supplement description in the text. Individual works of literature cited are the most important examples in English that are readily available in United States libraries. Paperbacks are marked with an asterisk (*).

General

Barnett, A. Doak. *Communist China and Asia.** New York: Vintage Books, 1961.

Chiang Monlin. *Tides from the West: A Chinese Autobiography.* New Haven: Yale University Press, 1947.

Chow Tse-tung. *The May Fourth Movement.* Cambridge: Harvard University Press, 1960.

Fairbank, John King. *The United States and China.** New York: Compass Books, 1962.

Lin Yutang. *From Pagan to Christian.* Cleveland: World, 1959.

——. *My Country and My People.* New York: Reynal & Hitchcock, 1935.

Snow, Edgar. *Red Star over China.** New York: Grove Press (Black Cat Series), 1961.

Literature

GENERAL

Hightower, James Robert. *Topics in Chinese Literature.* Cambridge: Harvard University Press, 1953.

Hsia, C. T. *A History of Modern Chinese Fiction.* New Haven: Yale University Press, 1961.

Ting Yi. *A Short History of Modern Chinese Literature.* Peking: Foreign Languages Press, 1953.

POETRY ANTHOLOGIES

Acton, Harold, and Ch'en Shih-hsiang (translators). *Modern Chinese Poetry.* London: Duckworth, 1936.

Payne, Robert (editor). *The White Pony: An Anthology of Chinese Poetry.** New York: New American Library, 1961.

PROSE ANTHOLOGIES

Clifford, William, and Milton, Daniel L. (editors). *A Treasury of Modern Asian Stories.** New York: Mentor Books, 1961.

Schyns, Joseph (editor). *1500 Modern Chinese Novels and Plays.* Peiping: Catholic University Press, 1948.

Snow, Edgar (editor). *Living China: Modern Chinese Short Stories.* New York: John Day and Reynal & Hitchcock, 1937.

Wang, Chi Chen (editor). *Stories of China at War.* New York: Columbia University Press, 1947.

Wu, Lucian (editor and translator). *New Chinese Short Stories.** Taipei: Heritage Press, 1962.

—— (editor). *New Chinese Writing.** Taipei: Heritage Press, 1962.

PROSE, INDIVIDUAL WORKS

Chao Shu-li. *Changes in Li Village;* translated by Gladys Yang. Peking: Foreign Languages Press, 1953.

Hsieh Ping-ying. *Girl Rebel: Autobiography;* translated by Adet and Anor Lin. New York: John Day, 1940.

Lao She. *Rickshaw Boy;* translated by Evan King. New York: Reynal & Hitchcock, 1945.

Lu Hsün. *Ah Q and Others: Selected Stories of Lusin*

[Lu Hsün]; translated by Chi Chen Wang. New York: Columbia University Press, 1941.

——. *Selected Works of Lu Hsün* (2 vols.). Peking: Foreign Languages Press, 1957.

Mao Tun. *Midnight;* translated by Hsü Meng-hsiung and A. C. Barnes. Peking: Foreign Languages Press, 1957.

——. *Spring Silkworms and Other Stories.* Peking: Foreign Languages Press, 1957.

Shen Ts'ung-wen. *The Chinese Earth;* stories translated by Ching Ti and Robert Payne. London: Allen & Unwin, 1948.

Ting Ling. *The Sun Shines over the Sangkan River;* translated by Yang Hsien-yi and Gladys Yang. Peking: Foreign Languages Press, 1954.

GENERAL

Theatre

Obraztsov, Sergei V. *The Chinese Puppet Theatre.* London: Faber, 1961.

Scott, A. C. *The Classical Theatre of China.* London: Allen & Unwin, 1956.

——. *Mei Lan-fang, Leader of the Pear Garden.* Hong Kong University Press, 1959.

Wimsatt, Genevieve B. *Chinese Shadow Shows.* Cambridge: Harvard University Press, 1936.

PLAYS

Kuo Mo-jo. *Chu Yuan, A Play in Five Acts.* Peking: Foreign Languages Press.

Lao She. *Dragon Beard Ditch.* Peking: Foreign Languages Press, 1956.

T'ien Han. *Kuan Han-ching, A Historical Drama.* Peking: Foreign Languages Press.

Ts'ao Yü. *Bright Skies;* translated by Chang Pei-chi. Peking: Foreign Languages Press, 1960.

——. *Thunderstorm;* translated by Wang Tso-liang and A. C. Barnes. Peking: Foreign Languages Press, 1958.

Music

Levis, John Hazedel. *Foundations of Chinese Musical Art.* Peiping: Vetch, 1936.

Opera

Ting Yi and Ho Ching-chih. *The White-Haired Girl.* Peking: Foreign Languages Press, 1953.

Painting, Architecture, Graphic Arts

Carter, Dagny. *Four Thousand Years of China's Art.* New York: Ronald Press, 1948.

Chang Ta-ch'ien. *Chang Da-chien, Chinese Painting with Original Paintings and Discourse on Chinese Art.* Hong Kong, 1961.

Chiang Yee. *Chinese Calligraphy.* Cambridge: Harvard University Press, 1954.

——. *The Chinese Eye: An Interpretation of Chinese Painting.* London: Methuen, 1935.

Chinese Woodcutters Association. *Woodcuts of Wartime China, 1937–1945.* Shanghai: K'ai-ming Book Co., 1946.

Hájek, Hoffmeister, and Rychterova. *Contemporary Chinese Painting.* London: Spring Books, 1961.

Hsü Pei-hung. *Hsü Pei-hung Album Sketches.* Peking: Peoples' Art Publishing House, 1958.

Roy, Claude. *Zao Wou-ki.* New York: Grove Press, 1960.

Speiser, Werner. *The Art of China: Spirit and Society.* New York: Crown Publishers, 1961.

Sullivan, Michael. *Chinese Art in the Twentieth Century.* London: Faber, 1959.

Willets, William. *Chinese Art** (2 vols.). London: Penguin, 1958.

Selected Articles in Journals

Birch, Cyril. "Chao Shu-li, a Writer of Contemporary China and His Background," *International PEN Bulletin*, Vol. II, No. 4, March 1952.

———. "Fiction of the Yenan Period," *China Quarterly*, October–December 1960.

———. "Lao She: The Humourist in His Humour," *China Quarterly*, October–December 1961.

Chao Mei-pao. "The Trend of Modern Chinese Music," *T'ien Hsia Monthly*, March 1937.

Chuin Ting. "Architecture Chronicle," *T'ien Hsia Monthly*, October 1937.

Hsü Kai-yu. "The Life and Poetry of Wen I-to," *Harvard Journal of Asiatic Studies*, December 1958.

Jen Ju-wen. "Art Chronicle," *T'ien Hsia Monthly*, February 1938.

Ling Tai. "Poetry Chronicle," *T'ien Hsia Monthly*, November 1938.

Mills, Harriet C. "Lu Hsün and the Communist Party," *China Quarterly*, October–December 1960.

Tu Heng. "Cinema Chronicle," *T'ien Hsia Monthly*, November 1938.

Wen Yuan-ning. "Art Chronicle," *T'ien Hsia Monthly*, September 1936.

Yao Hsin-nung. "Chinese Movies," *T'ien Hsia Monthly*, April 1937.

———. "Drama Chronicle," *T'ien Hsia Monthly*, September 1936.

"Great Plans for Education in China (Christian Universities Architecture)," *Far Eastern Review*, January–June 1920.

CHINESE

The following is a select list of background material to the text of this book and includes representative works of writers specifically discussed.

General

Hsien-tai Chung-kuo hsiao-shuo hsüan. Pai-hsin t'u-shu-wen chü kung-ssu, Hsiang-kang, 1960.

Liu Shou-sung. Chung-kuo hsin-wen hsüeh shih ch'u-kao. Tso-chia ch'u-pan-she, Peiching, 1956.

Wang Che-fu. Chung-kuo hsin-wen-hsüeh yün-tung shih. Chieh-ch'eng yin-shu chü, Shanghai, 1933.

Wang Yao. Chung-kuo hsin-wen-hsüeh shih kao. Hsin-wen-i ch'u-pan-she, Shanghai, 1953.

Ying-tzu (editor). Chung-kuo hsin-hsüeh shu-jen wu chih. Chih-ming shu-chü, Hsiang-kang, 1956.

Poetry

Ai Ch'ing. Ai Ch'ing shih-hsüan. Jen-min wen-hsüeh ch'u-pan-she, Peiching, 1953.

Hsü Chih-mo. Fei-leng-ts'ui ti yi-yeh. Hsin-yüeh shu tien, Shanghai, 1927.

Tsang Ke-chia (editor). Chung-kuo hsin-shih hsüan 1919–1949. Ch'ang-sheng ch'u-pan-she, Peiching, 1956.

Wen I-to. Wen I-to shih-wen hsüan-chi. Jen-min wen-hsüeh ch'u-pan-she, Peiching, 1953.

Prose

Chao Shu-li. Chao Shu-li hsüan-chi. K'ai-ming shu-tien, Shanghai, 1949.

Lao She. Lo-t'o hsiang-tzu. Ch'en-kuang ch'u-pan kung-ssu, Shanghai, 1949.

Lu Hsün. Ah Q cheng-chuan. Kuang-ming shu-tien, Shanghai, 1940.

Mao Tun. *Yeh-tzu.* K'ai-ming shu-tien ch'u-pan-she, Shanghai, 1933.

——. *Ch'ün-ts'an.* Ch'en-kuang ch'u-pan kung-ssu, Shanghai, 1949.

Pa Chin. *Chia.* Jen-min wen-hsüeh ch'u-pan-she, Peiching, 1955.

Ping Hsin. *Ch'ao-jen.* Ping Hsin ch'u-pan-she, 1951.

Shen Ts'ung-wen. *Pien-ch'eng.* K'ai-ming shu-tien, Shanghai, 1949.

Ting Ling. *Ting Ling wen-chi.* Ch'un-ming shu-tien, Shanghai, 1949.

Theatre

GENERAL

Ch'i Ju-shan. *Ch'i Ju-shan hui-i lu.* Chung-ying wu-kuang yin-she, Taipei, 1956.

Mei Lan-fang. *Mei Lan-fang wu-t'ai sheng-huo ssu-shih nien.* Jen-min wen-hsüeh ch'u-pan she, Peiching, 1952–54.

Ou-yang Yü-ch'ien. *Tzu wo yen-hsi i-lai, 1907–1928.* Chung-kuo hsi-chü ch'u-pan she, Peiching, 1959.

PLAYS

Lao She. *Lao She hsi-chü chi.* Ch'en-kuang ch'u-pan kung-ssu, Shanghai, 1949.

Ting Hsi-lin. *Ting Hsi-lin hsi-chü chi.* Wen-hua sheng-huo ch'u-pan-she, Shanghai, 1947.

Ts'ao Yü. *Lei-yü.* Wen-hua sheng-huo ch'u-pan-she, Shanghai, 1936.

——. *Ming-liang ti t'ien.* Hsi-chü ch'u-pan-she, Shanghai, 1956.

Cinema

Wang Tsu-lung. *Chung-kuo ying-chü shih.* Taipei, 1960.

Yang Ts'un. *Chung-kuo tien-ying san-shih-nien.* Shih-chieh ch'u-pan she, Hsiang-kang, 1954.

Painting and Graphic Arts

Ch'en Yen-ch'iao. *Lu Hsün yü mu-k'e.* K'ai-ming shu-tien, 1950.

Feng Tzu-k'ai. *Man-hua Ah Q cheng-chüan.* K'ai-ming shu-tien, Shanghai, 1939.

———. *Tzu-k'ai hua-chi.* K'ai-ming shu-tien, Shanghai, 1927.

Huang Mao-tzu. *Hua-chia Hsü Pei-hung.* Peiching ch'u-pan-she, 1953.

Music

Hsien Hsing-hai. *Yin-yüeh Hsien Hsing-hai.* Peiching ch'u-pan-she, 1957.

Nieh Erh. *Nieh Erh hua-chüan.* Yin-yüeh ch'u-pan-she, Peiching, 1957.

———. *Nieh Erh ko-ch'u hsüan-chi.* I-le ch'u-pan-she, Peiching, 1960.

Wang Kuang-ch'i. *Chung-kuo yin-yüeh shih.* Yin-yüeh ch'u-pan-she, Peiching, 1957.

Compilation on the Arts.

Li Pu-yüan, Li Shu-hua, Liang Te-so, Yang Ts'un-jen, and Cheng Chün-li. *Chung-kuo hsien-tai mei-shu shih.* Liang-yu t'u-shu yin shua kung-ssu, Shanghai, 1936.

INDEX

OTHER DOLPHIN BOOKS

ESSAYS AND LETTERS

Turquoise

OTHER DOLPHIN BOOKS

POETRY AND DRAMA

Purple